The Reclamation of Exmoor Revisited

Henry French • Leonard Baker
Ralph Fyfe

The Reclamation of Exmoor Revisited

Rethinking the Consequences of Nineteenth-Century Landscape Change

palgrave
macmillan

Henry French 🆔
University of Exeter
Exeter, UK

Leonard Baker 🆔
University of Bristol
Bristol, UK

Ralph Fyfe 🆔
University of Plymouth
Plymouth, UK

ISBN 978-3-031-81657-4   ISBN 978-3-031-81658-1   (eBook)
https://doi.org/10.1007/978-3-031-81658-1

This Palgrave Macmillan imprint is published by the registered company Springer Nature Switzerland AG.
The registered company address is: Gewerbestrasse 11, 6330 Cham, Switzerland

If disposing of this product, please recycle the paper.

FOREWORD

Since Exmoor was designated a National Park in 1954 and its limits were drawn on a map for the first time, we have become accustomed to its elongated shape stretching nearly from Ilfracombe in Devon to the west all the way to Minehead in Somerset to the east, an area of 264 square miles. But for a thousand years or more, Exmoor was known as a much smaller region focused on the old Royal Forest of Exmoor and the moorland commons that encircled it. It was indeed the moor around the headwaters of the great river Exe and its lesser-known, but more beautiful sister the river Barle (literally 'stream from the hills') which gave Exmoor its name.

Within today's National Park, this landscape still has a particular quality—an 'otherness'—ineffable, but without doubt a character that echoes that of the former Royal Forest, described by Westcote in 1630 as 'a spacious coarse barren and wild object, yielding little comfort by his rough complexion'. Almost uninhabited, inaccessible and often lawless, it must have been a forbidding place.

In 1815, the landscape of the old Royal Forest endured a seismic change when it was disafforested and fell into private hands, being acquired by the Knight family from Worcestershire. The Knight family's attempts to reclaim the wild moorland are at a scale that is too great to comprehend on the ground, but it was described by the agricultural economist Charles Orwin in 1929 as 'one of the greatest achievements ... that the nineteenth century has to show'. It was a colossal endeavour and an extraordinary landscape transformation, under a single family, in a relatively short period. Since then, our understanding of this part of Exmoor has been mainly through the prism of Orwin's work—A great scholar, but partial, nevertheless.

In *The Reclamation of Exmoor Revisited—Rethinking the Consequences of Nineteenth-Century Landscape Change*, Henry French, Leonard Baker and Ralph Fyfe bring a much needed and broader thinking to this subject and to this place. Against a backdrop of a 25-year surge in data about the archaeology of the Royal Forest and the physical nature of reclamation as well as the changing environment, they have combined rigorous historical research and the analysis of past environmental change to produce a compelling account of what the Knight family undertook between 1819 and 1897. The book explores the approach that the Knight family took to reclamation and the pivotal role of their tenants and offers a reassessment of their achievements.

The Royal Forest of Exmoor was a wild, 'other' place, and despite the huge changes wrought by the Knights, their labourers and their farming tenants, that wild quality still endures. Amidst the farmland, the neat beech hedges and the well-made roads, the roughness of Westcote's forest is still much in evidence. Like a semi-tamed beast, the landscape still shows its true self.

This new account provides the essential handbook to help us understand the heart of Exmoor and the people who shaped what we see today. Through this book, those nineteenth-century endeavours seem more extraordinary than ever.

Head of Access, Engagement and Estates   Rob Wilson-North
Exmoor National Park Authority, Dulverton, UK

PREFACE AND ACKNOWLEDGEMENTS

This volume is based on research funded by The Leverhulme Trust Research Grant RPG-2020-045 'A landscape transformed: the reclaiming of Exmoor Forest', for which Ralph Fyfe was Principal Investigator. The project ran between 2020 and 2022, with Henry French as Co-Investigator and Leonard Baker and Fran Rowney as post-doctoral researchers in history and palaeoecology, respectively. The project was designed to combine historical research in the newly rediscovered Knight estate archive with palaeoecological research at new levels of chronological resolution and sophistication. Research findings have been presented at COP26 in Glasgow in 2021, the British Agricultural History Society (BAHS) Spring Conference 2022, European Rural History Organisation (EURHO) conference in Uppsala June 2022, Exmoor National Park Archaeology Forum October 2022, European Social Science History (ESSH) conference in Gothenburg April 2023 and IUCN Peatlands Working Group/Global Peatland Initiative online symposium in September 2023. We are very grateful to participants at each of these events for their feedback. Aspects of this research have been published in articles in Agricultural History Review, Biodiversity and Conservation, Ecology and Evolution, Landscape Research, and Cultural and Social History.

We are particularly grateful for support during the project from Rob Wilson-North, Shirley Blaylock and Martin Gillard (Exmoor National Park Authority), particularly their expertise about the historical and archaeological evidence and for access to the Historical Environment Record; Morag Angus and colleagues in the Southwest Peatland Partnership for comments on the utility of the results for peatland restoration; U3A Minehead volunteers for transcribing the Knight Family Papers; Bette Baldwin and The Friends of Hoar Oak Cottage for digitising and transcribing the diaries and stocking records of Robert Tait Little; and to Pam and Peter Goodwin for their advice on Exmoor farming genealogies.

We would like to express our thanks to the following organisations for permission to publish images: Topfoto for Image 1, Chapter "Reassessing Reclamation Under John Knight, 1818–1842" from Punch magazine; the National Portrait Gallery for Image 1, Chapter "Frederic Knight and Robert Smith, 1843–1862" photograph of Frederic Knight; and the Merz Library collections for Image 2, Chapter "Frederic Knight and Robert Smith, 1843–1862" from JRASE 1856.

Exeter, UK	Henry French
Bristol, UK	Leonard Baker
Plymouth, UK	Ralph Fyfe

CONTENTS

ABBREVIATIONS

DHC   Devon Heritage Centre
EPG   Exeter and Plymouth Gazette
HA   Hectares
NDJ   North Devon Journal
SHC   Somerset Heritage Centre
SNA   The National Archives (Scotland)
TCWA   Taunton Courier and Taunton Courier and Western Advertiser
TNA   The National Archives (UK)
UKPP   UK Parliamentary Papers (Command Papers)
WSFP   West Somerset Free Press

LIST OF FIGURES

LIST OF IMAGES

LIST OF TABLES

Introduction

Abstract Exmoor has long featured in the history of agricultural development in England because of C. S. Orwin's pioneering history in 1929. In the last two decades, historians have noticed the emotive language and concepts used by contemporaries to describe and justify domestic reclamation and enclosure projects and have argued that these drew explicitly on ideas of colonisation. Recently, Carl Griffin has extended this 'domestic colonisation' narrative to the English enclosure movement, including Exmoor, but existing studies have said much less about how such ideas were put into practice, and with what effects. Rethinking reclamation on Exmoor is timely because recent projects on the landscape archaeology of 'improvement', and rapidly developing palaeoecological sampling techniques have expanded our knowledge of the chronology and effects of landscape change. In addition, in 2017, important documents from the Knight estate archive were rediscovered, which enabled a new research project to be undertaken on Exmoor's reclamation.

Keywords Agrarian history • Social history • Nineteenth-century Britain • Development • Enclosure • Colonial ideology • Landscape archaeology • Moorlands • Palaeobotany

NEW IDEAS ABOUT RECLAMATION

For more than a century, land reclamation has been part of a 'productivist' narrative of agrarian development in modern Britain, in which spectacular increases in soil fertility, yields and profits followed the application of new technology and farming methods—and justified its description as a 'revolution' in agriculture (Overton 1996: 1–7; Williamson 2002: 1–22). Conversely, there has been an equally long tradition of chronicling the negative social effects of these changes, notably the dispossession of small farmers and the immiseration of landless labourers (see J. L. & B. Hammond 1911). In both cases, though, these are stories of British exceptionalism: exceptional productivity or exceptional capitalist exploitation. Only in the last two decades has the British agrarian revolution been reinterpreted as part of a wider 'colonising' process, in which governing elites ought to impose new ideas about the ownership, value and productivity of land across the globe, often by systematic denigration of the knowledge, techniques and intentions of its existing users (Arneil 2012, 2019; Fisher 2022; Griffin 2023). Land reclamation fits particularly well into this new narrative, because it usually involved wholesale reconfiguration of the landscape, property rights and local populations and because its advocates required a powerful ideological commitment to 'progress' to off-set the heavy economic and social costs of such projects (Simpson 2022; Tindley 2009, 2010). Most recently, Carl Griffin has recast the history of enclosure and reclamation in these terms, as works of 'internal colonisation', and has included the reclamation of Exmoor by John and Frederic Knight within this account (Griffin 2023).

These exciting new ideas about the meanings and motives underlying agrarian change in nineteenth-century Britain provide the starting point for this study. We want to examine the strength of these 'colonising' ideals, particularly in motivating the efforts by Knights and their agents to enclose, drain and intensify land use on Exmoor between 1818 and 1897. However, we also want to apply new palaeoecological research methods, alongside new research on the historical sources, to assess the relationship between the rhetoric of improvement and the realities within the landscape of the estate itself. We will show that although Exmoor was undoubtedly 'colonised' by permanent settlers and new farming techniques in the nineteenth century, the process was neither wholly 'top-down', nor particularly extensive. Indeed, we will argue that the widespread public use of 'colonising' metaphors on Exmoor can obscure continuities in land use, and even de-intensification, in this period.

RECLAMATION AS INTERNAL COLONISATION

Despite the long English historiographical tradition of investigating the social costs of agrarian change, until the 1980s, agrarian historians and historical geographers tended to regard concepts such as 'reclamation' and 'improvement' as morally neutral technical terms, rather than ones that were ideologically charged (Whittle 2013; Thompson 2008). Historical geographers were the first to take a linguistic 'turn' towards unpicking the value-laden rhetoric behind ideas about landscape, such as the 'picturesque' (Cosgrove and Daniels 1988; Copley and Garside 1994; Daniels and Seymour 1990). More recently, historians have sought to understand the motivations, ideologies and discourses that spurred the ambitious 'improvement' projects witnessed during the late eighteenth and nineteenth centuries (Warde 2011; Finch and Giles 2007; Tarlow 2007: 67–89; Fisher 2022; Howkins 2014; Warde 2018; Griffin 2023), and how elite intellectual and social authority was projected onto landscapes and people through such campaigns.

As the fervour for agricultural 'improvement' grew, the moorlands of Exmoor came to be described within agricultural literature, popular newspapers and personal correspondence as a 'wild and deserted landscape' that had been 'abandoned' to a species of 'half-wild sheep' by an 'idle' local population whose customs, agricultural practices and mentalities were dangerously 'backward' and 'foreign' (Spender and Isaac 1858; Preston 1816: 35–39; Billingsley 1798: 286–9; Acland and Sturge 1851: 9–10, 159–60). For audiences of the period, such claims echoed assessments of distant 'primitive tribes', such as Native Americans, Africans or Australians. They took the concepts of 'cultivation' and 'civilisation' that had been connected during colonial encounters, and turned them 'inwards' against the 'idle' and 'immoral' rural poor who had created these 'unproductive' landscapes at home (Arneil 2012, 2019; Morera and Morgan 2019). This argument reverses earlier historical assumptions that 'the concept of exclusive property in land, as a norm to which other practices must be adjusted' was projected outwards through the British Empire, 'across the whole globe' (Thompson 1991: 163–4). Barbara Arneil has argued that the systematic demeaning of local peoples and practices is 'the theoretical and ideological framework by which ... colonisation is justified' (Arneil 2012). Indeed, in her study of 'domestic colonies' Arneil has argued that the ruling classes of Victorian Britain 'turned colonialism inwards' to 'solve the "problem" of marginalised populations' with proponents 'claiming the same economic and ethical "benefits" at home' as had been witnessed overseas (Arneil 2017: 1–5, 2019: 269–70). As Harris noted in his study of British Columbia, hostile polemics directed towards the native peoples' 'customary uses' of the landscape were lifted directly from the arguments first deployed against common land in England and Scotland (Harris 2004: 172; Jones 2019). Carl Griffin's recent examination of the discursive relationship between the development of 'internal colonialism' in England and the enclosure movement shows how this accompanied the push to reclaim the moorlands and other wastes. He argues that enclosers adopted the language of colonisation and sought to 'discredit and debase indigenous people; deny their agency and ability to manage the space and its resources' (Griffin 2023: 8–9). By recasting the rural poor as 'savage' or 'backward' agricultural improvers established their 'natural right … to exercise dominion over empty spaces' (Slack 2014: 31–2, 68). In fact, the rhetoric of 'enclosure' and 'improvement' could be applied equally in domestic or colonial contexts. Unfortunately, few studies of English agricultural improvement have examined the cultural, discursive and ideological connections between the late eighteenth- and nineteenth-century push for the reclamation of 'waste land' and colonial settlement, possibly because these were less directly state-sponsored than in other European countries (van der Grift 2015; Jones 2014). By contrast, the 'dialogue' between metropole and colonial 'periphery' has been examined very fruitfully in studies of other aspects of nineteenth-century government and culture (Potter and Saha 2015; Cooper and Stoler 1997). Recently, for example, John Watts has demonstrated how the politics of land reform in early-twentieth-century Britain was intimately connected to images of settling the 'imperial frontier' (Watts 2022).

Even so, the concept of 'internal colonialism' in Britain can sometimes function as an artificial or ahistorical metaphor. The concept was applied to the 'Celtic Fringe' during the 1980s, and its early proponents were criticised for emphasising the aspects that most resembled 'external colonialism', while minimising those that did not (Hind 1984; Chavez 2011; Hechter 1977). More recent studies avoid these 'artificial analogies' by focusing on how agricultural 'improvers' in Britain perceived, discussed and legitimised their activities as part of a global colonial effort. As Iain MacKinnon has argued in his assessment of the *Gàidhealtachd*, 'the language of colonization was widely expressed by government officials and agricultural improvers … they understood their work to be projects of colonization' (MacKinnon 2011, 2017). Other studies have added further nuance to such interpretations. Recent research on change in the Scottish Highlands by Tarlow and Jonsson has highlighted that although some writers and landlords were unremittingly hostile to cottars and subsistence farming, others sought to integrate locals within their colonial, paternalist visions of 'improvement' (Tarlow 2007: 78–87). Tarlow notes that clearances of tenants were supposed to be mitigated by the creation of new coastal fishing ports, to provide better incomes, housing and 'moral conditions' for those displaced from the countryside. It was the failure of these schemes that contributed to wholesale emigration, rather than the unrelenting prejudices of many landlords (Tarlow 2007: 85; Jonsson 2013). Similarly, Jonsson notes that after the failure of the British Fisheries Society, one strand of Enlightenment thought in Scotland focused on the 'colonial' resettlement of the Highlands in planned villages housing former cottagers and crofters, 'the aborigines of improvement in this country' (Jonsson 2013: 221). In this vision, the 'hardy' Highlander was regarded both as worthy of improvement but also possessed of rural virtues worth saving from urban degeneration in the 'rabbit warren' of London, and the 'pig-sty' of Edinburgh (Jonsson 2013: 220). Such views could not withstand either the costs of such resettlement schemes, or the assaults of unromantic advocates of political economy after 1800, but they illustrate that 'internal colonial' thinking could sometimes be aimed at redeeming or repurposing local populations, rather than simply dismissing or replacing them. Both strands of thought were applied to the people and landscapes of Exmoor at different points after 1818. Consequently, in this study, we will reexamine not only how cultural impetuses shaped the conduct of moorland reclamation 'on the ground' but also how the new landowners' preference for novel methods and external expertise led to the denigration and exclusion of the 'native' population of Exmoor and its agricultural knowledge (MacKinnon 2017; Griffin 2023; Arneil 2017; Tully 2008). By appreciating the power of these cultural discourses and moral impetuses, we can re-think these seemingly uneconomical and unsustainable attempts at landscape-scale reclamation (which previous scholars have sometimes attributed to ignorance or ineptitude).

Studies have also begun to question the environmental effects of such agrarian interventions. In 1999, James Winter drew parallels between reclamation on the Mendip Hills on the eastern flank of Somerset, and Exmoor. The enclosure of the Mendips was advocated by West Country improver, John Billingsley, in the same terms that he applied to Exmoor

(Winter 1999: 63–5; Williams 1971). The high plateaus were left as common grazing, on which 'an indifferent breed of sheep grazed on coarse grasses and provided an unenterprising community with mean livings', as Billingsley had observed on Exmoor (Winter 1999: 63; Billingsley 1798: 286–9). Unlike Exmoor, however, these upland pastures were quickly enclosed in the early nineteenth century and converted to tenanted arable farms during the high prices of the Napoleonic wars.

> … landowners and tenants … poured capital into draining, burning turf, breaking up the clay subsoil by deep plowing, constructing farm buildings and houses, and laying out 1,650 miles of hedges and stone walls (Winter 1999: 63)

However, they soon exhausted the soil, by preferring the quick-fix of lime to neutralise soil acidity, over the long-term investment in improved grasslands, higher stocking densities and better manuring. The uplands reverted to poor-quality summer grazing for livestock, interspersed with highly extractive potato grounds let to local miners and labourers, which further degraded the soil. The result was a landscape of ruined farmsteads and tumble-down stone walls, rather than one that testified to successful 'improvement'.

Nevertheless, huge areas of upland common grazing land were enclosed in the eighteenth and nineteenth centuries. Winchester estimates that between 2.1 and 2.3 million acres (0.84–0.93 m ha) were subject to Parliamentary enclosure after 1700, with a focus on the high moors after c. 1795, and 90 per cent of late enclosure acts (after 1845) referred to common 'wastes', mainly upland (Williamson 2002: 127–9; Winchester 2022: 134–5). However, he notes that only a portion of the land subject to enclosure statutes was usually fenced off behind dry-stone walls or hedges (Winchester 2022: 138–52). Substantial improvements to the soil to create improved grasslands were always expensive. It required paring rough grass, burning it, spreading the ashes, liming, manuring, drainage, and repeated ploughing, not to mention walling, shelter plantations and building farmhouses. In fact, upland enclosure was often initiated more to demarcate rights of grazing, mineral extraction or shooting than to create improved grasslands. Arable production on the higher moors tended to be transient and was not repeated after 1815, 'motivated by more optimism than good sense' (Williamson 2002: 133). Most famously, despite spending £210,000 on moorland reclamation at Kildonan (Scotland) between

1863 and 1881, the duke of Sutherland created only 3247 acres (1314 ha) of arable, three-quarters of which had dropped out of cultivation within a decade (Simpson 2022; Tindley 2009, 2010: 34–57). Indeed, Simmons notes that the reversion of upland enclosures to rough pasture was widespread between the mid-nineteenth and mid-twentieth centuries (Simmons 2003: 117–20). On Dartmoor, the area of rough pastureland increased by 6.3 per cent between 1885 and 1904 (Simmons 2003: 118). The 1930s Land Utilisation Survey found that 3 million acres (1.2 m ha) of moorland remained unenclosed, and one million acres (0.4 m ha) remained totally unfenced and presumably wholly unimproved (Williamson 2002: 135). Although only a limited acreage was fully 'improved' on Exmoor, little land reverted to rough grazing or heather moorland for shooting (Orr 1982: 28–50).

NEW UNDERSTANDINGS OF EXMOOR'S PAST

Historians have paid most attention to the reclamation of wetlands, particularly the draining of the fens, the Somerset Levels, and the mosses west of Manchester (Lindley 1981; Sharp 1982; Williams 1970; Hoyle 1992). This has only been redressed in the last 30 years (Winchester 2022; Williamson 2002: 115–38). There was one exception, though—the pioneering study of the reclamation of former Royal Forest of Exmoor, published by the agricultural economist, C. S. Orwin, in 1929 (Orwin 1929). Orwin had enjoyed many family holidays in the area, and this helped stimulate his professional interest in reconstructing the economic and agrarian effectiveness and profitability of the Knight family's campaign to enclose Exmoor in the nineteenth century (Orwin and Sellick 1970: 18–22). Orwin had access to estate documents and talked to protagonists who remembered developments in the latter years of Frederic Knight's ownership of the estate. Orwin wrote favourably about the transformation of the Exmoor Forest estate by the application of new technology (steam ploughs), new methods (liming and catch meadows), and new ideas and people (estate steward Robert Smith), depicting them as redolent of mid-Victorian optimism, but financially unsuccessful. He criticised the apparent failure of the original estate purchaser, John Knight, to achieve substantial agrarian change, and credited him instead with significant infrastructural investment (especially in drainage) that would pay off later. Orwin argued that the estate only became profitable in the 1870s and 1880s through sheep ranching, but this hardly outweighed the enormous sums that the Knights had spent on purchasing the estate and running it at a loss for 40 years. This cautionary interpretation echoed the judgements of later nineteenth-century observers but ensured that Exmoor featured as the primary example of upland 'improvement' when academic interest in British agrarian history emerged after World War II (Fussell 1948; French 2024).

In the last 50 years, detailed research in palaeobotany and landscape archaeology has produced dramatic increases in our understanding of Exmoor's development. Both approaches have supplemented the relatively limited documentary record (MacDermot 1973; Siraut 2009: 54–5). More sophisticated methods of dating and analysing the core samples of pollen obtained from the peat bogs on Exmoor have enabled reconstruction of the potential land use and plant species cover over 6000 years, or more. Similarly, since the 1990s, Exmoor National Park Authority's archaeological surveys of the surviving landscape features and physical remains across Exmoor have added much to our understanding of the farming regimes in place in the last 7–800 years (Siraut 2009: 11–27, 49–67).

The advent of radiocarbon dating has provided a much better understanding of the chronological sequences within palaeobotanical core samples. These are discussed in more detail in Chapter "Polemics and Practices", but this greater precision has provided a better understanding of the timing of changes on Exmoor, even if their causes are still debated. Most studies have agreed that although the clearance of tree cover began in the later Neolithic period, by the later Iron Age Exmoor, was largely a grass and heather-dominated moor, with significant signs of cereal crops as well. This pattern echoed those in other upland regions such as South Cumbria, Lancashire and Wales (Fyfe et al. 2003: 228). There has been a decisive move away from the idea that Exmoor suffered a dramatic population collapse, because of emigration to Brittany, after the end of the Roman occupation (Moore et al. 1984). As Riley and Wilson-North have cautioned, though, 'contemporary archaeological evidence for life on post-Roman Exmoor is practically non-existent', with virtually no detectable settlement archaeology, and very little investigation of the area's contemporary hillforts (Riley and Wilson-North 2001: 85; Francis and Slater 1990: 21–2).

Later studies have found no evidence of a significant increase in woodland regeneration, or scrub, on Exmoor after the fifth century, unlike on Dartmoor and Bodmin moors (Fyfe and Davies 2011: 19). Rippon et al.

have suggested that on Exmoor at least, the transition to the mediaeval period represented the first significant alteration in land use since the late Iron Age (Rippon et al. 2006: 35). Until the tenth century, the existing pattern of dispersed settlements, or individual farmsteads, and extensive grasslands persisted. From that point, there was much more evidence of cereal pollen particularly on the favourable south-facing slopes of southern Exmoor. Its presence implies greater levels of cereal cultivation because such pollen is not dispersed widely, and its concentrations were sufficient to indicate cropping rather than wind-borne distribution (Rippon et al. 2006: 53). However, most of the sites also show continuing evidence of pastoral flora.

The presence of both pastoral grazing and arable production suggests that by the Norman Conquest, many settlements were practicing an in-field/out-field system of 'convertible husbandry'. This enabled periodic cropping of the out-field (lower) moors, during which turf was pared off the surface, burned and the alkali ashes ploughed into the acidic moorland soil. It was then sown for two or three years in succession, particularly with rye, and then put down to pasture again for 5 or 10 years, before being ploughed again (Rippon et al. 2006: 55). This 'extensive' system of crop rotation was recorded in the area in thirteenth-century sources. It enabled the demands of a growing population and the restricted acreages of in-field ridge-and-furrow strips to be balanced against the limited fertility of nutrient-poor acidic upland soils (Gilliard 2003: 188–93). While this did not create tightly organised village settlements, it implies a greater degree of communal farming practice than is evident in the Romano-British period. Ridge-and-furrow strip fields remain visible on Molland Common, Withypool Hill and Common and at Winsford Hill, bordering the forest (Riley and Wilson-North 2001: 126).

It was in this period that the first evidence also emerges of Exmoor's place as a Royal Forest, at the centre of a concentric circle of rights. Although this royal status may have preceded the Conquest, after it, most of the greater Exmoor area was placed under Forest law, amounting to perhaps 150,000 acres (60,703 ha) (Hegarty and Wilson-North 2014: 11–12). After Magna Carta (1215), Forest law applied only to the Royal Forest, with grazing rights distributed to the 'suitors' residing in the 13 surrounding parishes, whose commons bordered the moor. Over time, landholders in the surrounding parishes began to encroach piecemeal onto the commons. The Black Death accelerated this process of consolidation and abandonment of holdings, and the subsequent retreat from the moorland margins between the fifteenth and late sixteenth centuries, as at Badgworthy (Riley and Wilson-North 2001: 94–8).

The palaeobotanical record lends some support to documented changes about which historians have been sceptical. In 1637, a witness in a court case alleged that in recent years, the number of sheep pastured annually in summer on Exmoor had declined from 43,000 to 16,000, because of a rise in grazing charges (Hallam 1978). Fifteen years later, a witness from South Molton stated that the quality of Exmoor pastures had declined, because now there were insufficient sheep to keep down the coarse grasses. While Hallam could find no evidence that stocking rates on Exmoor or its environs fell below 1.5 sheep per acre (0.6 ha) per year (or 3 acres/1.2 ha for the summer months), the palaeobotanical record shows more evidence of grazing pressure on non-arboreal richness and concentrations of fungal spores from animal dung at test-sites in the sixteenth and early seventeenth centuries, than in the eighteenth or even early nineteenth centuries (Rowney et al. 2023: 6). Certainly, the documentary record suggests that in 1736 sheep numbers in the forest totalled 37,400, if all the rights were exercised, 13,941 from tenants in the bordering settlements and 16,195 from 'strangers' (who hired rights to pasture in the forest) (MacDermot 1973: 394). The total number given by the Enclosure Commissioners in 1814 was 32,000 sheep (MacDermot 1973: 409). This relative stability may reflect the exercise of a greater level of control on stocking densities by the Forest lessees in the eighteenth century compared to the early seventeenth, perhaps because they wanted to extract higher charges.

Recent research on the landscape archaeology of 'improvement' and reclamation on Exmoor in the nineteenth century has also revealed the sheer scale of the Knights' ambitions. Aerial photographic surveys have revealed that over 200 kms of drains were cut across Exmoor after 1818, particularly on the slopes north and south of Simonsbath around Emmett's Grange immediately south of Simonsbath, and on the moorland plateau of The Chains to the north (Hegarty and Wilson-North 2014: 33–8). There were several phases of drainage: the first under John Knight in the 1820s and 1830s, including the creation of the much larger Pinkery Canal; the second, under his son Frederic, accompanied the creation of many of the farms on Exmoor in the 1840s, plus work to maintain and extend earlier networks (Riley and Wilson-North 2001: 139–42; Jamieson 2002; Siraut 2009: 130–4; Pugsley 2017). These drains were intended to lower the water table in boggy areas, divert natural springs into water courses, and (in some cases, as at Emmett's Grange) create catch meadows by allowing water to run across south-facing slopes to promote early grass growth in spring. Although their efficacy was limited, modern inventories highlight the concentration and sheer number of drains cut in the central, western and northern forest and emphasise commitment shown by Knights and their tenants to large-scale reclamation.

NEW RESEARCH OPPORTUNITIES

By reconceptualising 'reclamation' as an ideologically charged, and even neo-colonial enterprise, historians have helped explain why contemporaries were prepared to set their sights on lands that appeared as unpromising as Exmoor, and why they persisted when these lands proved so intractable. This interpretative insight has the potential to explain two lacunae in Orwin's research on Exmoor: firstly, why John Knight was prepared to pay so much for the Royal Forest and spend so much on it for so little apparent reward; and secondly, why his son ploughed on through so many false-starts, failed schemes and financial losses. We can only understand why Exmoor was enclosed if we look beyond the language of agrarian and economic utility towards rhetoric which stressed the 'redemptive' power of improvement (on lands and peoples), the 'law-like' inevitability of capitalist development, and the moral imperative to impose such schemes, if necessary, by displacing the existing inhabitants.

Although aerial photography and large-scale archaeological surveys have shown the extensive 'earthworks' of improvement, there also remains considerable scope to assess the ecological and botanical impact of 'improvement'. Put simply, did enclosure and improvement really have as much effect on Exmoor as its proponents claimed in the nineteenth century? We need to look beyond the archival records to refine earlier research on the palaeobotanical record by focusing more precisely on the nineteenth century, and on sites that were subject to reclamation efforts. Such analyses offer the opportunity not merely to assess the extent of the change in hydrology, flora and stocking densities but also to assess the relative significance of each of these changes. More sensitive methods of measuring Carbon 14 also allow much more precise dating of these sequences of change.

CONTEXT OF RESEARCH WITHIN MODERN
ECOLOGICAL RESTORATION

Current concerns about ecological restoration create an extra impetus to researching the history of the Knights' tenure and transformation of the Royal Forest. Exmoor has been in the vanguard of landscape-scale peatland restoration programmes since the late 1990s, with nineteenth and twentieth-century drainage schemes cast as processes that significantly altered the 'ecosystem services' delivered by these landscapes (Grand-Clement et al. 2013). Restoration practices seek to make reparations for past alterations to these complex systems, and thus enhance the contribution that such systems can make to important societal agendas, including supply of clean water, mitigation of climatic change, and maintenance of biodiverse systems (Holden et al. 2007). Classical restoration ecology practice elevates historical ecosystems as targets against which to measure the success of restoration efforts; however, it has always been difficult to establish the nature of such 'optimum' historical states (or when they existed) (Hobbs et al. 2011). On Exmoor, drainage has been cited as the primary driver of change over the last two centuries, but this implies that the basepoint for restoration should be its condition immediately prior to that drainage. An alternative would be to seek comparable undamaged (un-reclaimed) landscapes as models, but given the extent of enclosure and use of UK uplands, this is rarely possible.

At present, like many disturbed ecosystems, there is little information about Exmoor's pre-disturbance state (for argument's sake, the condition of the moorland in the late eighteenth century), or a full account of the processes by which it was transformed thereafter. As already described, landscapes such as Exmoor have long histories of land use stretching back millennia: by the late eighteenth century, Exmoor was already heavily transformed. Current ecological restoration should thus be informed by a long durée understanding of the evolution of the ecosystems, and the processes of land use and land use change that created the current situation, to support good decision-making in the future (Higgs et al. 2014). This does not mean slavishly recreating the past, but we must understand the trajectories that ecosystems have followed and, thus, their likely future directions.

THE REDISCOVERY OF THE KNIGHT FAMILY ARCHIVE

Finally, in 2017, another new research opportunity appeared. After several years of enquiries, Rob Wilson-North, Head of Access, Engagement and Estates at Exmoor National Park Authority, located a large collection of historical documents in the hands of a descendant of the Knight family (Wilson-North 2018). The most important were account books from the time of John Knight, particularly 'No. 1 Exmoor Account Book' covering Knight's first year on the estate in 1819–1820. Orwin does not appear to have seen this, and it illustrated how quickly John Knight initiated changes to transform the estate, as Chapter "Reassessing Reclamation Under John Knight, 1818–1842" will explain. The collection also included later accounts for 1839–1841, at the end of John Knight's involvement on Exmoor, and substantial amounts of correspondence between Frederic Knight and his father, between 1841 and 1850, and between Frederic and his stewards Robert Smith (covering 1848–1862) and Frederic Smyth (covering 1862–1870), and detailed estate accounts from 1852 onwards. While Orwin had used some of the accounts and materials between Frederic Knight and Robert Smith, the estate accounts provided more information about the estate in its final 30 years in the Knights' hands. These rediscoveries offered a unique opportunity to place this enriched documentary archive alongside more sophisticated palaeobotanical research methods, to establish the extent and intensity of the reclamation of Exmoor, to reconsider its chronology, and think in new ways about the motives for such an endeavour.

REFERENCES

PRIMARY PRINTED SOURCES

Acland, T., and W. Sturge. 1851. *The Farming of Somersetshire*. London: John Murray.

Billingsley, J. 1798. *General View of the Agricultural of Somerset, with Observations on the Means of its Improvement*. Bath: R. Cruttwell.

Preston, R. 1816. *A Review of the Present Ruined Condition of the Landed and Agricultural Interests*. London: Law and Whittaker.

Spender, E., and T.W.P. Isaac. 1858. The Labourer. *Journal of the Bath and West of England Society* 6: 130–177.

SECONDARY WORKS

Arneil, B. 2012. Liberal Colonialism, Domestic Colonies and Citizenship. *History of Political Thought* 33 (3): 491–523. https://www.jstor.org/stable/26225797.

———. 2017. *Domestic Colonies: The Turn Inward to Colony*. Oxford: Oxford University Press. https://doi.org/10.1093/oso/9780198803423.001.0001.

———. 2019. The Failure of Planned Happiness: The Rise and Fall of British Home Colonies. In *Happiness and Utility: Essays Presented to Frederic Rosen*, ed. G. Varouxakis and M. Philp, 269–288. London: UCL Press. https://doi.org/10.2307/j.ctvf3w1s5.18.

Chavez, J.R. 2011. Aliens in their Native Lands: The Persistence of Internal Colonial Theory. *Journal of World History* 22 (4): 785–809. https://www.jstor.org/stable/41508018.

Cooper, F., and A. Stoler. 1997. *Tensions of Empire: Colonial Cultures in a Bourgeois World*. Berkeley: University of California Press. https://www.jstor.org/stable/10.1525/j.ctt1pp03k.

Copley, S., and P. Garside, eds. 1994. *The Politics of the Picturesque. Literature, landscape and aesthetics since 1770*. Cambridge: Cambridge University Press.

Cosgrove, D., and S. Daniels, eds. 1988. *The Iconography of Landscape. Essays on the symbolic representation, design and use of past environments*. Cambridge: Cambridge University Press.

Daniels, S., and S. Seymour. 1990. Landscape Design and the Idea of Improvement. In *An Historical Geography of England and Wales*, ed. R.A. Dodgshon and R.A. Butlin, 487–520. London: Academic Press. https://r2.vlereader.com/Reader?ean=9781483288413.

Finch, J., and K. Giles, eds. 2007. *Estate Landscapes: Design, Improvement and Power in the Post-medieval Landscape*. Woodbridge: Boydell Press.

Fisher, J. 2022. *The Enclosure of Knowledge: Books, Power and Agrarian Capitalism in Britain, 1600–1800*. Cambridge: Cambridge University Press. https://doi.org/10.1017/9781009049283.

Francis, P.D., and D.S. Slater. 1990. A Record of Vegetational and Land-Use Change from Upland Peat Deposits on Exmoor. Part 2: Hoar Moor. *Proceedings of the Somerset Archaeological and Natural History Society* 134: 21–22.

French, H. 2024. The Wild West of England': Enclosure, Stag-hunting, and the Creation of New Popular Perceptions of Exmoor in the Nineteenth Century. *Cultural and Social History* 21 (4): 507–534. https://doi.org/10.1080/14780038.2024.2359502.

Fussell, G.E. 1948. "High Farming" in Southwestern England, 1840–1880. *Economic Geography* 24 (1): 53–73. https://doi.org/10.2307/141039.

Fyfe, R., and H. Davies. 2011. The Pattern of Vegetation Development on Exmoor. *Proceedings of the Somerset Archaeological and Natural History Society* 154: 11–22.

Fyfe, R.M., A.G. Brown, and S.J. Rippon. 2003. Mid- to late-Holocene Vegetation History of Greater Exmoor, UK: Estimating the Spatial Extent of Human-induced Vegetation Change. *Vegetation History Archaeobotany* 12 (4): 215–232. https://www.jstor.org/stable/23417996.

Gilliard, M. J. 2003. The Medieval Landscape of the Exmoor Region: Enclosure and Settlement in an Upland Fringe. Unpublished Ph.D. thesis, University of Exeter.

Grand-Clement, E., K. Anderson, D. Smith, D. Luscombe, N. Gatis, M. Ross, and R.E. Brazier. 2013. Evaluating Ecosystem Goods and Services After Restoration of Marginal Upland Peatlands in South-West England. *Journal of Applied Ecology* 50 (2): 324–334. https://doi.org/10.1111/1365-2664.12039.

Griffin, C. 2023. Enclosure as Internal Colonisation: The Subaltern Commoner, Terra Nullius and the Settling of England's "Wastes". *Transactions of the Royal Historical Society* 33: 95–120. https://doi.org/10.1017/S0080440123000014.

van der Grift, L. 2015. Introduction; Theories and Practices of Internal Colonization. The Cultivation of Lands and People in the Age of Modern Territoriality. *International Journal for History, Culture and Modernity* 3, 2: 139–158. https://doi.org/10.18352/hcm.480.

Hallam, O. 1978. Vegetation and land use on Exmoor. *Proceedings of the Somerset Archaeology and Natural History Society* 122: 37–51. https://sanhs.org/wp-content/uploads/06Hallam.pdf.

Hammond, J. L. & B. 1911. *The Village Labourer 1760–1832: A Study in the Government of England before the Reform Bill*. London & New York: Longmans, Green.

Harris, C. 2004. How Did Colonialism Dispossess? Comments from an Edge of Empire. *Annals of the Association of American Geographers* 94 (1): 165–182. https://www.jstor.org/stable/3694073.

Hechter, M. 1977. *Internal Colonialism: The Celtic Fringe in British National Development, 1536–1966*. Berkeley: University of California Press.

Hegarty, C., and R. Wilson-North. 2014. *The Archaeology of Hill Farming on Exmoor*. Swindon: English Heritage.

Higgs, E., D.A. Falk, A. Guerrini, M. Hall, J. Harris, R.J. Hobbs, S.T. Jackson, J.M. Rhemtulla, and W. Throop. 2014. The Changing Role of History in Restoration Ecology. *Frontiers in Ecology and the Environment* 12: 499–506. https://doi.org/10.1890/110267.

Hind, R.J. 1984. The Internal Colonial Concept. *Comparative Studies in Society and History* 26 (3): 543–568. https://www.jstor.org/stable/178555.

Hobbs, R.J., L.M. Hallett, P.R. Ehrlich, and H.A. Mooney. 2011. Intervention Ecology: Applying Ecological Science in the Twenty-first Century. *BioScience* 61: 442–450. https://doi.org/10.1525/bio.2011.61.6.6.

Holden, J., L. Shotbolt, A. Bonn, T.P. Burt, P.J. Chapman, A.J. Dougill, E.D.G. Fraser, K. Hubacek, B. Irvine, M.J. Kirkby, M.S. Reed, C. Prell,

S. Stagl, L.C. Stringer, A. Turner, and A. and F. Worrall. 2007. Environmental Change in Moorland Landscapes. *Earth Science Reviews* 82: 75–100. https://doi.org/10.1016/j.earscirev.2007.01.003.

Howkins, A. 2014. The Use and Abuse of the English Commons, 1845–1914. *History Workshop Journal* 78: 107–132. https://www.jstor.org/stable/43299028.

Hoyle, R.W. 1992. Disafforestation and Drainage: The Crown as Entrepreneur. In *The Estates of the Crown, 1558–1640*, ed. R.W. Hoyle, 353–388. Cambridge: Cambridge University Press.

Jamieson, E. 2002. Archaeological Survey Work at Larkbarrow Farm. *Proceedings of the Somerset Archaeological and Natural History Society* 146: 17–26. https://sanhs.org/wp-content/uploads/Jamieson.pdf.

Jones, E.B. 2014. The Rural "Social Ladder": Internal Colonization, Germanization, and Civilizing Missions in the German Empire. *Geschichte und Gesellschaft* 40 (4): 457–492. https://www.jstor.org/stable/24368716.

Jones, H. 2019. Property, Territory and Colonialism: An International Legal History of Enclosure. *Legal Studies* 39 (2): 187–203. https://doi.org/10.1017/lst.2018.22.

Jonsson, F.A. 2013. *Enlightenment's Frontier: The Scottish Highlands and the Origins of Environmentalism*. New Haven and London: Yale University Press. https://doi.org/10.2307/j.ctt5vkrjr.

Lindley, K. 1981. *Fenland Riots and the English Revolution*. London: Heinemann Educational Books.

MacDermot, E.T. 1973. *A History of the Forest of Exmoor*. Newton Abbot: David & Charles.

MacKinnon, I. 2011. "Eachdraidh nar cuimhne" – "History in our memories": An Analysis of the Idea that the Highlands and Islands of Scotland can be Understood as a Site of Colonisation. Unpublished PhD Thesis, University of Ulster.

———. 2017. Colonialism and the Highland Clearances. *Northern Scotland* 8: 22–48. https://doi.org/10.3366/nor.2017.0125.

Moore, P.D., D.L. Merryfield, and M.D.R. Price. 1984. The Vegetation and Development of Blanket Mires. In *European Mires*, ed. P.D. Moore, 203–235. London: Academic Press. https://doi.org/10.1016/B978-0-12-505580-2.50010-6.

Morera, R., and J. Morgan. 2019. Marshland Drainage: A Colonial Project? A Comparison of France and England in the Early Modern Period, trans. L. Gleeson. *Études Rurales* 203 (1): 42–61. https://www.jstor.org/stable/27055294.

Orr, W. 1982. *Deer Forests, Landlords and Crofters. The Western Highlands in Victorian and Edwardian Times*. Edinburgh: John Donald Publishers.

Orwin, C.S. 1929. *The Reclamation of Exmoor Forest*. London: Oxford University Press.

Orwin, C.S., and R.J. Sellick. 1970. *The Reclamation of Exmoor*. Newton Abbot: David & Charles.

Overton, M. 1996. *Agricultural Revolution in England. The transformation of the agrarian economy 1500–1850*. Cambridge: Cambridge University Press. https://doi.org/10.1017/CBO9780511607967.

Potter, S.J., and J. Saha. 2015. Global History, Imperial History and Connected Histories of Empire. *Journal of Colonialism and Colonial History* 16 (1): 1–31. https://doi.org/10.1353/cch.2015.0009.

Pugsley, S. 2017. Exmoor and the Picturesque. *Exmoor Review* 58: 76–81.

Riley, H., and R. Wilson-North. 2001. *The Field Archaeology of Exmoor*. Swindon: English Heritage.

Rippon, S.J., R.M. Fyfe, and A.G. Brown. 2006. Beyond Villages and Open Fields: The Origins and Development of a Historic Landscape Characterised by Dispersed Settlement in South West England. *Medieval Archaeology* 50: 31–70. https://doi.org/10.1179/174581706x124239.

Rowney, F.M., R.M. Fyfe, L. Baker, H. French, M.B. Koot, H. Ombashi, and R.G.O. Timms. 2023. Historical Anthropogenic Disturbances Explain Long-term Moorland Vegetation Dynamics. *Ecology and Evolution* 13 (3): 1–17. https://doi.org/10.1002/ece3.9876.

Sharp, B. 1982. *In Contempt of all Authority: Rural Artisans and Riot in the West of England, 1586–1660*. Berkeley: University of California Press.

Simmons, I.G. 2003. *The Moorlands of England and Wales: An Environmental History 8000BC to 2000AD*. Edinburgh: Edinburgh University Press.

Simpson, D. 2022. Culmaily, a Model of Improvement: Reform, Resistance and Rationalisation in South-eastern Sutherland. In *Land Reform in the British and Irish Isles since 1800*, ed. S. Evans, T. McCarthy, and A. Tindley, 27–47. Edinburgh: Edinburgh University Press. https://doi.org/10.3366/edinburgh/9781474487689.003.0002.

Siraut, M. 2009. *Exmoor: The Making of an English Upland*. Chichester: Phillimore & Co.

Slack, P. 2014. *The Invention of Improvement: Information and Material Progress in Seventeenth-Century England*. Oxford: Oxford University Press. https://doi.org/10.1093/acprof:oso/9780199645916.001.0001.

Tarlow, S. 2007. *The Archaeology of Improvement in Britain, 1750–1850*. Cambridge: Cambridge University Press. https://doi.org/10.1017/CBO9780511499708.

Thompson, E.P. 1991. *Customs in Common*. London: Merlin Press. https://ebookcentral.proquest.com/lib/exeter/reader.action?docID=4563562&ppg=104.

Thompson, S. 2008. Parliamentary Enclosure, Property, Population and the Decline of Classical Republicanism in Eighteenth-Century Britain. *Historical Journal* 51 (3): 621–642. https://www.jstor.org/stable/20175187.

Tindley, A. 2009. "The Iron Duke": land reclamation and public relations in Sutherland, 1868–95. *Historical Research* 82 (216): 303–319. https://doi.org/10.1111/j.1468-2281.2007.00441.x.

———. 2010. *The Sutherland Estate, 1850–1920: Aristocratic Decline, Estate Management and Land Reform.* Edinburgh: Edinburgh University Press. https://doi.org/10.1515/9780748642670.

Tully, J. 2008. The Struggles of Indigenous Peoples of and For Freedom. In *Public Philosophy in a New Key. Vol. 1: Democracy and Civil Freedom*, ed. J. Tully, 257–289. Cambridge: Cambridge University Press.

Warde, P. 2011. The Idea of Improvement, c. 1520–1700. In *Custom, Improvement and the Landscape in Early Modern Britain*, ed. R.W. Hoyle, 127–148. Aldershot: Ashgate Publishing. https://r1.vlereader.com/Reader?ean=9781351946643.

———. 2018. *The Invention of Sustainability: Nature and Destiny, c. 1500–1870.* Cambridge: Cambridge University Press. https://doi.org/10.1017/9781316584767.

Watts, J. 2022. Land Reform, Henry Rider Haggard, and the Politics of Imperial Settlement, 1900–1920. *Historical Journal* 62 (2): 415–435. https://doi.org/10.1017/S0018246X21000613.

Whittle, J. 2013. Introduction: Tawney's Agrarian Problem Revisited. In *Landlords and Tenants in Britain, 1440–1660: Tawney's Agrarian Problem Revisited*, ed. J. Whittle, 1–18. Woodbridge: The Boydell Press. https://www.jstor.org/stable/10.7722/j.ctt31nh5b.9.

Williams, M. 1970. *The Draining of the Somerset Levels.* Cambridge: Cambridge University Press.

———. 1971. The Enclosure and Reclamation of the Mendip Hills, 1770–1870. *Agricultural History Review* 19 (1): 65–81. https://www.jstor.org/stable/40273415.

Williamson, T. 2002. *The Transformation of Rural England. Farming and the Landscape 1700–1900.* Exeter: University of Exeter Press.

Wilson-North, R. 2018. The Rediscovery of the Knight family archive and its importance to Exmoor. *Proceedings of the Somerset Archaeological and Natural History Society* 161: 189–194. https://sanhs.org/wp-content/uploads/2020/08/15-R-Wilson-North.pdf.

Winchester, A.J.L. 2022. *Common Land in Britain. A History from the Middle Ages to the Present Day.* Woodbridge: The Boydell Press. https://doi.org/10.2307/j.ctv2fl smcz.

Winter, J. 1999. *Secure from Rash Assault: Sustaining the Victorian Environment.* Berkeley: University of California Press. https://doi.org/10.2307/jj.5973214.

Reassessing Reclamation Under John Knight, 1818–1842

Abstract Contemporary observers applied the language of 'internal colonisation' to Exmoor, arguing explicitly that there was a moral imperative to reclaim a landscape that had been misused and neglected by its 'slovenly' local inhabitants. They praised the sale of the Royal Forest in 1818 to Midlands iron-founder John Knight as an opportunity to redeem the land for the national interest by applying superior external knowledge, personnel and capital. The chapter charts how Knight embarked on a wholesale transformation of Exmoor. However, because these efforts did not produce obvious or swift results, they were downplayed by contemporaries and later historians. The chapter uses the rediscovered estate archive to emphasise the potentially radical scope of John Knight's schemes, and how they embodied 'colonial' thinking.

Keywords Agrarian history • Social history • Nineteenth-century Britain • Colonial ideology • Domestic colonies • Development • enclosure • Moorlands • Landscape archaeology • Drainage

By the turn of the nineteenth century, the presence of 'waste land' across Britain had become a pressing social and political issue. As John Wagstaffe explained in 1805, to ensure 'economic prosperity' and 'moral health', 'the numerous millions of waste acres which yet disfigure our nation must become a widely extended garden, replete with every useful production congenial to our climate' (Wagstaffe 1805). The food crises of the Napoleonic Wars, the new Board of Agriculture and the increasing popularity of agricultural societies had fostered a desire to enact landscape-scale 'improvement' projects (Winchester 2022; O'Donell 2015; Mingay 1997; Turner 1980). Moreover, the British state had emerged from the Napoleonic Wars as a confident, proactive and repressive vehicle for the landowning aristocratic establishment (Poole 2019; Eastwood 1997). Under these influences, the Royal Forest of Exmoor (22,000 acres/8903 ha) was disafforested and enclosed in 1815 and then sold to the Knight Family in 1818. Driven by this improving fervour, almost all the landscape-scale drainage, irrigation, infrastructure, fertilisation and mining projects on Exmoor occurred between the purchase of the Royal Forest by John Knight in 1818 and the dismissal of the Frederic Knight's most influential land agent, Robert Smith, in 1862 (Riley 2019). This period has since formed the core of modern histories because of the dramatic narratives of personal misfortune, social conflict and agricultural 'revolution' that it provoked (Siraut 2009; Burton 1989). However, until the recent rediscovery of the Knight Family's estate papers, accounts and correspondence, most assessments of 'reclamation' were wholly reliant on agricultural commentators and second-hand observers. By utilising these new documents, Chapters "Reassessing Reclamation Under John Knight, 1818–1842" and "Frederic Knight and Robert Smith, 1843–1862" will reassess when and how many of the most famous acts of landscape change, such as mass drainage and irrigation, were conducted. Equally, these papers provide insight into the lives, work and struggles of the men and women who were actually tasked with 'improvement' on Exmoor, whose history has been overlooked by previous 'top down' approaches to agricultural history (Fig. 1).

Combining these new archival documents with an assessment of the cultural pressures to 'improve' and 'civilize' Exmoor prompts a reconsideration of the tenures of both John Knight (1818–1843) and Frederic Knight (1843–1897). Within existing studies of nineteenth-century reclamation, Robert Smith's stewardship under Frederic Knight (1848–1862) has garnered the most attention. According to Orwin and Sellick:

> the years 1851 to 1861 mark the most active and important period in the story of Exmoor reclamation. Practically all the farms were made and occu-

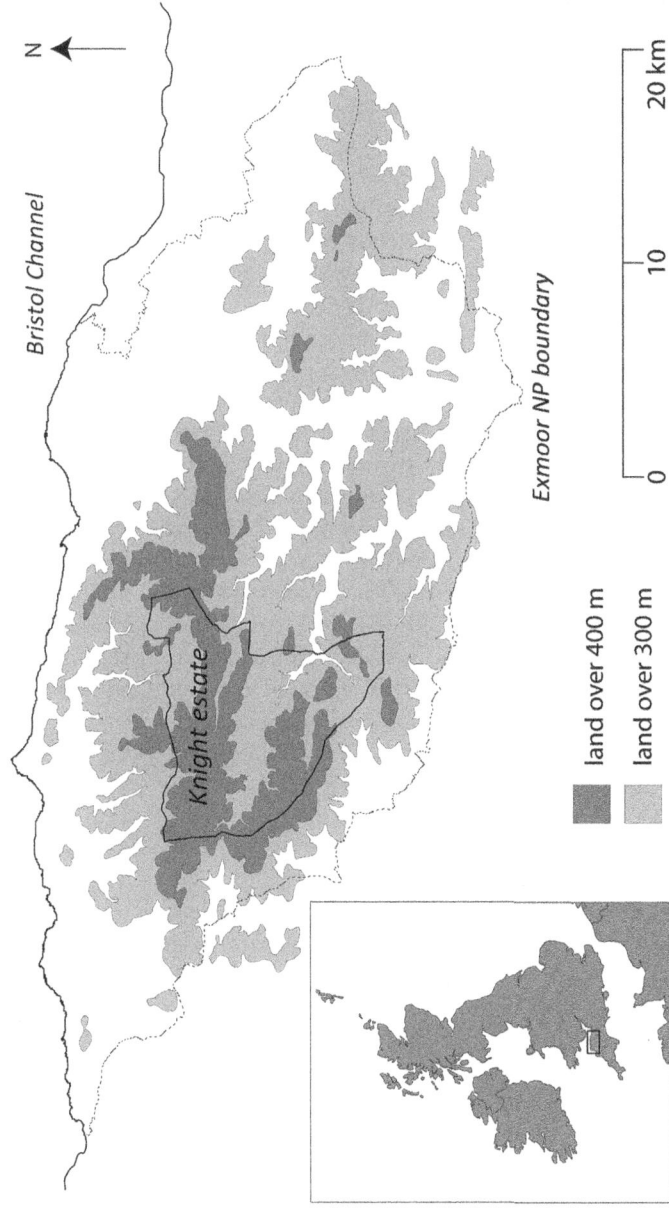

Fig. 1 Extent of the estate purchased by John Knight, within the boundary of the modern Exmoor National Park

> pied during this time; tenants came, and unfortunately went; the system of
> farming which was ultimately to succeed began to be evolved. (Orwin and
> Sellick 1970: 114)

Undoubtedly, this was an important period, encompassing both the height of 'high farming' on Exmoor and the estate's most fervent adoption of the discourses of 'internal colonialism'. However, it has also ensured that the work of John Knight has been frequently misunderstood, misattributed or underestimated. For their assessment of this earlier period, Orwin and Sellick were largely reliant upon observations from later commentators, most notably Thomas Dyke Acland's assessment of 1851 and Samuel Sidney's history of reclamation on Exmoor published in 1878 (Acland and Sturge 1851; Sidney 1878). However, Acland and Sidney drew their information from Robert Smith, who had a professional interest in publicising his own achievements (SHC A/EJM/1/1/6 Frederic Knight to John Knight, 6 January 1850). Consequently, both concluded that John Knight's primary contribution to the reclamation of Exmoor had been the road network. In all other areas, Sidney argued, his 'lavish' plans had been defeated by a 'climate that made corn-growing at any price unprofitable', leaving the estate to flounder until Smith arrived (Sidney 1878). Yet, the new documents about John Knight's efforts in the 1820s reveal that instead of being an overly optimistic and haphazard 'improver', he devised a series of interlocking schemes that provided the foundations for all the reclamation projects witnessed during the nineteenth century.

Conducting a focused case study of reclamation on Exmoor also provides new insight into how the discourses and practices of 'internal colonialism' operated. As Griffin acknowledges, studies of these discourses have yet to 'delineate the influence such thinking had on the projectors of actual enclosure' (Griffin 2023; Irvine 2015). Similarly, scholars of colonial North America have noted that if our aim is to understand colonialism rather than simply 'the imperial mind', then it is essential to investigate how these strategies were given material form 'on the ground' (Harris 2004). As will be demonstrated throughout this chapter, casting the previous inhabitants as ignorant savages unable to cultivate land and the moorland as an empty or valueless *tabula rasa* encouraged landowners, land agents and tenant farmers to engage in experimental and untested reclamation schemes. Using the Knight family's correspondence and papers, we can assess how the discourses and ideologies of 'internal colonialism' evolved outside of elite literary circles and its influence on the day-to-day implementation of reclamation.

INTERNAL COLONIALISM AND THE IDEOLOGIES
OF IMPROVEMENT

Although this section will focus on the discourses that influenced reclamation schemes on Exmoor, the Knight family also had explicit colonial connections of their own. John Knight's mother was Henrietta Cunningham, daughter of Daniel Cunningham of St Kitts, a notorious 'sugar baron' and slaveowner (Atkins 2014: 36–7; Fowler 2020). Although the precise details are unclear, because Henrietta was not referenced explicitly in her father's will, it seems likely that a portion of the family's wealth was sourced from the slave trade (Legacy of British Slavery Database, n.d.). However, by 1818, John Knight's primary sources of income were his ironworks in Wolverley, a series of estates near Kidderminster and Bromsgrove, Birmingham, and a large mortgage contracted in the belief that he would soon inherit Downton Castle from his uncle, Richard Payne Knight (Orwin and Sellick 1970). Furthermore, throughout this period, the Knights also had direct contact with another form of 'overseas exploitation' through their in-laws in Ireland. Through John Knight's second wife, Jane (nee Allanson-Winn), the family were connected to the Lords Headley of County Kerry. Although Lord Headley was praised by British commentators as 'one of the best landlords in the county', his successors would become renowned for the harsh treatment of their Irish tenants and labourers (MacMahon 2017; Lucey 2011). The Knights visited Ireland frequently, and the two families discussed reclamation via a long series of correspondence (SHC A/EJM/1/3/2 George Allanson-Winn to John Knight, 7 June 1821; SHC A/EJM/1/1/3 John Knight to Frederic Knight, 2 March 1833; SHC A/BAZ/1/5 Lord Headley to Frederic Knight, 14 April 1839). Lord Headley took an active interest in the improvement of Exmoor, providing strategies, techniques and labour for ongoing projects. Such intimate networks of knowledge, labour and finance indicate the interlocking nature of 'internal' and 'external' colonialism (Griffin 2023; Arneil 2020).

The discourses that legitimised and encouraged the creation of a 'home colony' on Exmoor through the exclusion of local people were taken directly from the philosophical justifications of early colonialism in North America. Since the late seventeenth century, the writings of John Locke on property had provided the principal foundations for colonisation. According to Locke, indigenous hunter-gatherer land use constituted and created 'waste' that was antithetical to the 'notion of value' (Arneil 2012;

Turner 2018; Neocleous 2012). Building upon these views, it was argued that indigenous peoples' 'inability' to cultivate the land reflected inherent moral or intellectual failings that provided grounds for dispossession. As Locke argued in 1690:

> God gave the world to Men in Common … [but] it cannot be supposed he meant it should always remain common and uncultivated. He gave it to the use of the Industrious and Rational (Locke 1988: 118).

Even during these early encounters, parallels were drawn between the Native Americans and the 'idle poor' across Britain. For example, the 'pastoral savagery' of the Irish was juxtaposed against markers of 'English civility' such as 'cultivation and enclosure' during the plantation of Ireland (Montaño 2011; Griffin 2023). Consequently, supporters of reclamation on Exmoor had centuries of discursive tradition to draw upon. For example, the *North Devon Journal* argued that:

> There seems a great stir upon the forest; improvement is rapidly on the march there; cultivation is reaching the hill tops … The old forest will soon become a civilized district. (*NDJ*, 9 November 1843)

It was the intimate connection between the active cultivation of land and the advance of civilised society that enabled the discourses of colonialism to return across the Atlantic during the seventeenth and eighteenth centuries. By the nineteenth century, agricultural and social improvement had become almost inseparable.

Building upon these philosophies, for many commentators, the lack of cultivation meant that Exmoor was considered *terra nullius*. In their analyses, the moorlands were presented as an inherently fertile but unutilised and 'empty' space. In 1798, John Billingsley described Exmoor as a 'useless and void space' whilst advocating for enclosure as it 'would train up a rising generation to care and industry, instead of theft and idleness' (Billingsley 1798: 286–289). Despite being used for centuries for seasonal grazing, the lack of permanent settlement, infrastructure and visible cultivation ensured that agricultural writers consistently complained that Exmoor consisted of '20,000 acres seemingly abandoned to a backward species of half-wild sheep' (Spender and Isaac 1858). As a writer for the *Morning Chronicle* stated, Exmoor was one of the few spots left in England 'where the works of creation appear in the sternness of their original mould, unchanged by the art and industry of man' (*Morning Chronicle*, 10 August 1849). Although this may have pleased sportsmen or romantic poets, for agricultural writers, such abandonment was horrifying, considering the latent fertility of the moorland. In his assessment, Philip Pusey provided one of the most succinct arguments for 'internal colonialism':

> you find the heath growing knee-high—a proof that the land has strength; you frequently find tall ferns … an unfailing sign that the land has depth as well as goodness, and wherever ferns grow wheat might be reaped. But there is a wonderful indifference in the owners to the use of land. (Pusey 1853: 309)

These discourses echoed Locke's condemnations of the Native Americans who had been supposedly provided with 'all the comforts of life' in their native soils but had squandered it 'for want of improving it by labour' (Irvine 2015; Arneil 2019). Such language not only condemned the local population as idle and unfit to hold such fertile territory but also presented the landscapes of Exmoor as engines of agricultural productivity that could be easily reclaimed and remade into a productive farm-scape.

As the belief in Exmoor's untapped fertility grew, so too did direct comparisons with 'foreign' locales. In particular, the image of the 'frontier' was repeatedly invoked by writers who wished to stress both the dangerous or alien nature of these landscapes and their wasted potential. Samuel Sidney claimed that Exmoor was as 'wild and desolate as an American prairie, until it was disafforested by Act of Parliament in 1818' (Sidney 1878: 72). Similarly, a reporter for the *Morning Post* stated that 'this strange, wild and remote piece of country … reminds one of the prairies of western America' (*Morning Post*, 10 August 1863) whilst the *London Evening Standard* concurred that Simonsbath appears 'like a rugged outlaw settlement in the midst of a vast prairie' (*London Evening Standard*, 7 August 1867). Reports of ongoing reclamation projects on Exmoor also used this imagery, with the *North Devon Journal* drawing the parallel very explicitly:

> The Red Men of North America have already succumbed before the dread fire-water, and the red deer are certain in their turn to bow their antlered heads before Mr Robert Smith and his water meadows. (*NDJ*, 4 October 1860)

By using the emotive language of 'the frontier', proponents of reclamation ensured that these landscapes were remade into a 'virgin' territory that could be reformed by 'knowledgeable' settlers. Indeed, during this period, any sufficiently distant, dangerous or 'untouched' landscape could be invoked to depict the moors as a colonial 'other'. In the *Illustrated London News*, for example, the reporter stated that 'no sheep-station in Australia could seem more utterly desolate' than Simonsbath (*Illustrated London News*, 22 October 1853). The *Western Times* similarly argued that in terms of its 'sparse terrain' and 'potential for cultivation' the 'Forest of Exmoor' held as much promise as 'the richest lands of South America', ensuring that 'all parties should proceed to settle these lands with hope … although much progress has not yet been made' (*Western Times*, 10 July 1847; c.f. *Wolverhampton Chronicle*, 26 December 1832). In newspapers and agricultural literature, Exmoor was thus remade into a colonial space, and the campaign for its improvement was compared to the efforts to civilise and 'improve' similar regions across the globe.

If the landscapes of Exmoor were being transfigured into foreign and dangerous locations, then a similar process was also enacted upon local people. As the study of folklore and 'local custom' became increasingly prevalent during the late eighteenth and nineteenth centuries, the inhabitants of Exmoor were identified as uniquely superstitious and backward. The 'educational' pamphlet, *An Exmoor Scolding*, purported to give its readers the opportunity to learn the 'uncouth expressions and barbarous words and phrases' that accompanied an 'Exmoor Courtship'. According to the preface of the ninth edition, previous copies had proven 'of some use to those Lawyers who go to Western Circuit' as the Exmoor 'language' was spoken only by 'the lowest class of people in the county' who were 'more uncouth and barbarous than even the worst among the Devonians' (Lock 1746/1792: iii-vi). Such distrust and censure continued throughout the following century. In his history of the region, F. J. Snell described the moors as being 'the favourite resort of the hunted, proscribed and outlawed', leading to the population becoming 'completely savage'. Similarly, their laws and society were marked by a 'savage vindictiveness' that was only 'tamed' with the arrival of the Knights (Snell 1903: 91, 67). As Christine Hardyment has argued, writers have typically used moorland to 'look into history, rather than towards progress' (Hardyment 2012). Yet, during the nineteenth century, this literary device was used to present the people of Exmoor as uniquely ignorant and incapable of managing the land. As one reporter concluded in 1841:

that the moor is cultivable there can be no doubt; those spots whereat this has been attempted and persevered with present decisive evidence of what may be done, but the work of general regeneration has not yet been set about ... its people being deficient in that penetration which is the property of a mind enlightened by science, and which could not fail, did it but exist, to throw the most cheering light on those operations which may hereafter be commenced. (*Kerry Examiner,* 20 August 1841)

Although the backwardness and ignorance of local people was often used for comical effect by regional newspapers, these supposed character traits were not perceived as harmless (c.f. *Dundee Courier,* 5 March 1844; *Devizes & Wiltshire Gazette,* 11 January 1844). Instead, these men and women were presented as impediments to agricultural improvement on Exmoor (Image 1).

The arguments that the local people were uniquely ignorant were reinforced through comparisons to 'savage' populations overseas. In contrast to other areas of Britain, where the racialisation of the rural poor legitimised institutions such as Poor Laws, Exmoor 'colonial analogies' remained fixated on land use and cultivation (Griffin 2020; Fowler 2020). In the *North Devon Journal,* it was claimed that Exmoor had remained 'wild and uncultivated', meaning that its population 'have not to fly like

PROFESSOR BUCKWHEAT EDUCING THE AGRICULTURAL MIND.

Image 1   'Professor Buckwheat educing the Agricultural Mind'. (Source: *Punch,* vol. 9, no. 216, 8 August 1845, p. 98)

the aborigines of America at the approach of civilization' (*NDJ*, 8 September 1853). Similarly, Thomas Dyke Acland commented that the 'native hill-countrymen of Exmoor' possessed:

> slovenly habits of primitive farming and a limited circle of ideas … He is like a foreigner, living many miles from a market town, with the sea on the north and the Forest surrounding him; he has, therefore, comparatively few opportunities for intercourse with others and is chiefly dependent for his ideas on the traditions of former generations. (Acland and Sturge 1851: 159–60)

Importantly, in these descriptions, it was the unimproved landscapes of Exmoor that had caused the rural poor of this region to remain backward and 'foreign'. Samuel Sidney argued that the lack of roads and outside connections meant that the population of Exmoor in 1815 were the descendants of 'smugglers and poachers, and female fugitives from the law of settlement'. This ensured that 'cultivation was miserable in the extreme' and that 'a man who had been seen hoeing a field of [turnips] was pronounced a madman for destroying his own produce' (Sidney 1878). The people of Exmoor were not merely remnants of a primitive English past but fundamentally different, and more dangerous, than their lowland neighbours.

In public debates and newspaper articles regarding the 'land question', Exmoor residents were placed alongside other 'problem' populations as being incapable of governing their own land (Cragoe 2010; Bull 2010). In 1833, the region was described as like the 'South and West of Ireland' comprising 'the most sterile and barren districts of the country'. In these landscapes:

> a turf hovel is tenanted by a half-savage people; and this desolate region, and these aboriginees [sic] are by far the greater proportion of the counties Cork, Kerry and Galway and on the plains of Exmoor and Dartmoor … The native who 'cultivates' this soil, tenanting from one to ten acres (over a hundred of which, that hunger-baned diminutive animal, which they call a cow, ranges in vain for subsistence). (*Public Ledger & Daily Advertiser*, 28 December 1833)

In such descriptions, the rural poor of Exmoor were equated to Irish labourers. As the century progressed, the intertwining of race, folklore and custom became increasingly explicit. The *London Evening Standard* claimed that they possessed the 'appearance and customs ... some attribute to the early-British' (*London Evening Standard*, 7 August 1867). Similarly, the *Exeter Flying Post* concluded that Exmoor 'marked a boundary between Britons and the English' and that the moorland had since been occasionally inhabited by 'the English colonisers of Somerset and Devon', but the local population had not been tamed as 'traces of them are by no means extinct, especially in the wilder parts of the country' (*Exeter Flying Post*, 20 August 1873). By the late nineteenth century, local folklorist Alice King had detected physical traces of this Celtic connection:

> The dwellers of Exmoor and in its neighbourhood are in many respects a race apart. They have often the dark hair and eyes which give an almost southern type to the people of North Devon, their accent has something French about its peculiar intonation ... (King 1884: 305)

Through such descriptions, the natives of Exmoor were separated from their neighbours in Somerset and Devon. By presenting them as a more barbaric, savage and potentially pseudo-Celtic 'race', these discourses legitimised their ongoing exclusion and replacement by more advanced and civilised farmers who could supposedly tame Exmoor.

Such depictions of Exmoor and its inhabitants encouraged serious consideration by local and national authorities of the plantation of a 'home colony'. For elites in provincial England, this promised to cure many ongoing social problems. During the Swing Riots, the Bishop of Bath and Wells presented a petition to the House of Lords from the people of Frome claiming that due to a lack of 'productive employment' the rural poor were 'in a wretched state of dependence for the necessaries of life', but this could be overcome 'by diverting the application of these outcasts from manufacture to agriculture for their own support, under strict regulations'. To achieve this:

> It would be beneficial to the distressed districts of the county of Somerset ... if a home colony were established, on uncultivated lands, under strict regulations, which have already been tried with success, to encourage industry and skilful agriculture, and to enable the poor to maintain themselves with more comfort than their present condition permits. (*England in 1830* 1831: 95–8)

In 1835, this 'home colony' proposal would be resurrected through a series of articles in local and national newspapers, which would identify the 'uncultivated lands' as Exmoor. This new campaign would expand upon the 'strict regulations' stating that 'public houses will be excluded from the colony—that spirits will not be allowed—persons guilty of drunkenness to dismissed therefrom'. Similarly, 'the men are not to be allowed to bring their wives and children … until a large number of acres should be cultivated', and certain plots should be left aside as a 'boon to experienced and well-deserving workmen' in the form of their own allotments (*Sun*, 10 June 1835; *Devizes & Wiltshire Gazette*, 18 June 1835). Evidently, both the 1830 petition and 1835 articles were founded upon John Billingsley's argument in 1798 that the improvement of Exmoor 'would train up a rising generation to care and industry, instead of theft and idleness' (Billingsley 1798: 286–289). Although these 'home colony' proposals had been rendered obsolete by John Knight's purchase, their presence served to reinforce the discourses of internal colonialism (*Dorset County Chronicle*, 18 June 1835). As in colonial regimes elsewhere, the 'improvement' of land was believed to be the best route to civilise the local population (Bhandar 2018).

Moreover, for many, a 'home colony' on Exmoor would not only benefit the West Country but also improve the entire nation's economic and moral prospects. As Arneil has noted, proponents of 'domestic colonies' often presented their plans as the moral alternative to costly acts of 'foreign imperialism' (Arneil 2017: 13–15). This point was made explicitly in a debate regarding potential military interventions in North America:

> Let them see if they could not cultivate and enclose first the waste lands they had got at home, rather than go to a distant country for them … There was Salisbury Plain, cultivate that, and the Wiltshire Downs, and Dartmoor, and Exmoor, and a good many more moors. (*Norfolk News*, 14 February 1846)

In this instance, the established comparisons between Exmoor and the American frontier served to benefit the 'anti-imperialists'. At the same time, it was argued that the 'improvement' of Exmoor would prevent the ongoing emigration of farmers to the colonies by providing them with a landscape where 'the industrious application of their labour and capital may be profitable' (*West Briton & Cornwall Advertiser*, 24 July 1818; *Bristol Mercury*, 30 September 1843). In these discourses, the reclamation and improvement of Exmoor was depicted as an issue of international importance. By improving these moorlands, the Knight family not only had the opportunity to 'civilize' the local population and create a valuable estate from 'virgin' land, but their work also had the potential to save the nation and earn universal acclaim.

RECLAMATION UNDER JOHN KNIGHT, 1818–1842

With the powerful invectives against 'valueless' moorlands and immoral locals beginning to circulate, John Knight's purchase of Exmoor from the Crown in 1818 for £50,000, alongside his subsequent acquisition of neighbouring allotments and the manor of Brendon for similarly exorbitant sums, was met with surprise but also widespread praise. Although his bid was ten times that of the next highest bidder, Sir Thomas Dyke Acland, the belief that Knight could 'reclaim' the moor was widespread (Orwin and Sellick 1970: 41–59). According to the *Bath Chronicle*:

> Under the judicious direction of this gentleman, and with his ample fortune, this vast and hitherto uncultivated tract of country will shortly assume a new and cheerful character. A handsome residence is in the course of erection, and great improvements of the soil are in contemplation, which, from the undoubted fertility of the greater part of this extensive Moor, will not fail yielding its spirited proprietor a valuable compensation. (*Bath Chronicle*, 14 October 1819)

For John Knight, the key to achieving this 'new and cheerful' character was maintaining complete control over every aspect of reclamation and cultivation. At the heart of his plans for 'improvement' was a system of 'demesne-farming'. Although this approach to agriculture is primarily associated with mediaeval England, it had been kept alive by Anglo-Irish landlords such as the Headleys. In essence, 'demesne-farming' meant that the entire estate was managed as single agricultural entity with the landowner directing day-to-day business (Stone 2005; Fitzpatrick 2018; Lucey 2011). Consequently, Knight refused to accept tenants or let out any land as farms. All 'improvement' and 'cultivation' would be conducted by waged labourers 'barracked' in a disparate series of cottages that followed the design of 'Scottish Bothies'. John Knight intended to oversee all reclamation projects from a rented property in Lynmouth and then Simonsbath House. As he would later explain, this approach to improvement emerged from a desire to 'establish my family' on Exmoor, which necessitated complete control over every aspect of reclamation (SHC A/BAZ/1/5 John Knight to Charles Knight, 30 December 1841) (Image 2).

Image 2   Exmoor boundary fence. (Source: Rob Wilson-North and the Exmoor National Park Authority)

To ensure that his plans could be achieved, John Knight first sought to privatise the formerly 'open' Royal Forest, legally and materially. Although there were no permanent inhabitants on the Royal Forest, with the only structure built prior to 1818 being Simonsbath House, enclosure still displaced locals and disrupted lives (Siraut 2009). As scholars of mediaeval and early modern Exmoor have shown, those living on the fringes of the moorland had long exercised common rights to pasturage and fuel on the Royal Forest. Officially, commissioners surmised that the enclosure of the Royal Forest in 1815 dispossessed 52 'free suitors from ancient tenements' in the parishes of Withypool and Hawkridge; approximately 100 'Suitors at Large' from the other parishes that ringed the moorland, and many hundreds of 'Strangers', a term used to describe individuals from parishes within ten miles of the Royal Forest who paid a fee either to the crown or a suitor to temporarily gain pasture rights (NA CRES/2/1503 Exmoor Inclosure Reports; Gillard 2002: 206–7; MacDermot 1973: 180–210, 278–285; Siraut 2009: 88–100; Fox 1991: 303–323). While these rights had become commercialised by the eighteenth century, with enclosure commissioners reporting the loaning of rights to 'Strangers' from as far afield as Dorset, the opening of Exmoor between April and October remained a cornerstone of local life (NA CRES/2/1503 Exmoor Inclosure Reports). Between 1814 and 1817, the Deputy Forester's accounts reveal that on average 27,578 sheep were pastured on the moor by 442 'Free Suitors' and 'Strangers', primarily from North Molton, Porlock and Swimbridge, but encompassing 59 North Devon parishes (NA LR/5/1/2 Accounts of William Lock). To combat these individuals, John Knight announced in regional newspapers that the presence of any 'foreign' animal on the moorland was now an act of 'malicious trespass' (*TCWA*, 22 October 1818, 29 October 1818, 15 April 1819). These were not empty threats, because he pursued legal action in ways that even his relatives thought were excessive (SHC A/EJM/1/3/2 George Winn to John Knight, 7 June 1821). These legal threats and cultural redefinitions were reinforced by substantial material transformations. To cement his claims physically upon the moorland, one of John Knight's first priorities in 1819 was the construction of a boundary wall, or 'Ring Fence', that encircled the entirety of the Royal Forest and extended for 30 miles. Coupled with his plan for demesne-farming, the new wall furthered John Knight's goal of separating Exmoor from the rest of the region.

John Knight's early improvement schemes were heavily influenced by the notion of the moorland being *terra nullius*. In contrast to later nineteenth-century assessments, which claimed that 'much time was lost' under John Knight and that landscape-scale reclamation only 'commenced upon the superintendence of Mr Robert Smith', the new evidence reveals that multiple schemes for reclamation were enacted during these initial years (Acland and Sturge 1851: 28–9; Darby 1873: 105–6). In a letter to his wife, Knight acknowledged that he had an overabundance of projects: 'full of my plans as usual; perhaps when you return you will find too many of them executed' (SHC A/BAZ/1/5 John Knight to Jane Knight, August 1826). Indeed, John Knight did not arrive on Exmoor as an amateur. As an agricultural survey of Worcestershire reveals, his farm at Lea Castle was managed in a 'capital and spirited style', with 159 acres (64 ha) of turnips, barley, wheat, carrots and vetches, the rest pasture, meadows, woods and plantations. He had also 'made experiments on folding sheep for both wheat and barley ... he uses lime and soot plentifully' (Pitt 1810: 26–7). In addition, through his first wife John Knight had been introduced to Scottish agriculture. In 1826, he claimed that Falkirk, Stirlingshire, was 'the finest [city] imaginable and the country round it in the finest state of cultivation and more and better planted that any part of England' (SHC A/BAZ/1/5 John Knight to Jane Knight, 12 October 1826). On Exmoor, John Knight sought to merge his previous successes with contemporary Scottish farming, albeit with a larger focus on drainage and irrigation due to the region's 'boggy soils'. The existence of a 'master plan' is revealed by frenzied pace of improvement between 1819 and 1821. Before his purchase had been finalised, Knight entered into an agreement with neighbouring landowner, Sir Thomas Acland so that he could 'commence the drainage of the peat lands' from 1 May (SHC A/EJM/1/3/1 Richard Strong to John Knight, 21 March 1819). However, the accounts for 1819 to 1821 reveal that after being allowed access, Knight started far more. Between May and December 1819, he initiated construction of the ring fence, roads, canals, water-carriages, drains and cottages; carrying out repairs to Simonsbath House; and quarrying stone and lime. In early 1820, he had begun building a manor house at Simonsbath; enclosing and building Cornham and Honeymead Farms; and building Hoar Oak Cottage (SHC A/EJM/3/3/1 Exmoor Abstract No. 1). Although dangerously optimistic and expensive, the feverish work of these initial years suggests that Knight had clear intentions and a firm belief in reclamation.

Previous historians have focused on the most visible outlay of labour and capital, the roads. Although it is undeniably impressive that John

Knight laid 22 miles of new road between 1819 and 1821 across a moorland where even dirt tracks had been a luxury, the rediscovery of the estate's earliest accounts reveals that this work was dwarfed by concomitant irrigation and drainage projects (Orwin and Sellick 1970: 39–56). According to 'Exmoor Abstract No. 1', in his first three years on Exmoor, John Knight focused on cutting open drains on the largest areas of peatland, namely The Chains, Exe Head and Hearlake. On Exmoor, 'open' drainage usually took the form of 'gutters from 4 to 7 feet deep and from 20 to 30 feet apart' (Acland and Sturge 1851: 13). Of note, on The Chains 1843 cubic yards (1409 m³) were cut during June 1819 on the 'North Side', which were then deepened and expanded in November 1819 and December 1819. Contemporaneously, on 'Exhead', 36 perch (181 m) of open drains were cut, which were then supplemented by 12 other smaller drains in the following months. The open drains on Hearlake were also repeatedly cut and expanded over a period of three months between June and August 1819 (SHC A/EJM/3/3/1 Exmoor Abstract No. 1; Baker et al. 2023). These geographically focused open drainage schemes were joined by a widespread series of 'undersoil drainage' projects dotted around the estate. In contrast to 'open drainage', undersoil or 'thorough drainage' involved inserting a drain underground and then covering it with rubble and soil (Robinson 1986). In his initial years, John Knight installed these drains at: Ferny Ball, Hereliving, Hoare Oak, Picked Stones, Red Stone Hill, Simonsbath House, West Gate, Goat Hill, Duredon, the Warren, Wester Emmetts, Cranescombe, Brendon Common, Prayway, Benjamy, and Winnaway (SHC A/EJM/3/3/1 Exmoor Abstract No. 1). Consequently, the geographical patterns of drainage suggest that in his initial plan for Exmoor, John Knight had clearly demarcated different areas of the moor for pastoral and arable farming. The 'open' or 'surface' drains were carefully planned to work with the topography as a means of improving the moorland grass for pasture. Conversely, 'undersoil drains' were meant to take water away from potential arable fields without disrupting the landscape (Riley 2019: 34–5, 52–3). Evidently, prior to his arrival on the moorland, John Knight accepted the popular perception of Exmoor's peatland as having a hidden fertility that could support vast 'improved' pastures and intensive wheat farming.

Accompanying these drainage projects were a series of interlocking and supporting irrigation schemes. Described in the original accounts as 'contour leets' or 'water-carriages', these channels were designed to support the creation of new pastures through either standard irrigation or water-meadows. On Exmoor, there had been a tradition of 'floating' or 'catch-water meadows' which used a system of channels to pass a continuous, moving film of water through the meadow sward at certain times of the year. This reduced the 'hungry gap' between the exhaustion of winter fodder, and the new spring growth, which was crucially important during the short growing seasons on Exmoor (Cook and Williamson 2007). Between 1819 and 1821, the most significant water-carriage built by John Knight was labelled as the 'Pinkery, Hearlake-Goat Hill-Driver Water-Carriage'. Beginning at a headwater stream for the Barle River, it ran along the south of Pinkery to the current Driver Farm. It was recorded as being 1026 perch (5160 m) long and is believed to have been 2 m wide and 0.5 m deep with a 3.1 m bank on either side (SHC A/EJM/3/3/1 Exmoor Abstract No. 1). Importantly, parts of this water-carriage were constructed alongside the drains on Hearlake and Pinkery suggesting that these may have been interlocking systems intended to carry overflow water and mud from drainage projects to help with the irrigation and fertilisation (Riley 2019: 35–9). Smaller water-carriages were also situated on Halscombe and Woolcombe, Little Ashcombe, Great Ashcombe, Cloven Rock Cottage, Cornham and Honeymead Farms, and the 'Tythe Allotment' (modern-day Lanacombe, Trout Hill, Pinfords, Swap Hill, Kittuck and Madacombe). The positioning of these smaller water-carriages indicates that John Knight intended for there to be a 'central band' of intensive pastoral or mixed farming that ran through the upland hills of Pinkery, Hearlake, Goat Hill and Driver. In turn, these would be supported by the vast pastures created by 'open drainage' on areas such as The Chains, whilst 'thorough drainage' would create pockets of arable land across Exmoor that could easily be accessed and fed upon by animals to fulfil the stratagems of 'high farming' (Fussell 1948).

Alongside the landscape-scale drainage and irrigation schemes, potentially the most ambitious project conceived during these early years was the Pinkery Canal. According to the 'Exmoor Abstract', this was dug between October 1819 and March 1820 and was meant to connect to 'the Warren Canal' built between November 1819 and March 1820. The Pinkery Canal ran for 9 km along the north side of the River Barle from the heart of The Chains to just south of Warren Farm, on the 450-m contour line. Meanwhile, the Warren Canal ran along the same contour on northern side of the Exe Valley, from Exe Head in the west to Rams Combe in the east, a total length of approximately 7.5 km (A/EJM/3/3/1 Exmoor Abstract No. 1). Both canals were to be fed by the artificial

'Pinkery Pond', which was dug at some point prior to 1830 (Riley 2019: 30–1). Recent archaeological surveys have concluded that these canals were intended to be part of a vast infrastructure network to underpin the reclamation of some of the most inaccessible areas of moorland. At Warren Farm, the canal's eastern terminus, there is evidence of railway tracks that would have travelled north-east to the harbour at Porlock Weir, just outside the Knight estate (SHC DD/BR/bn/31 John Knight to Charles Bailey 1826–1827). This connection would have allowed the easy transportation of building materials and artificial fertilisers to the heart of John Knight's improvement operations whilst also permitting the export of crops and livestock (Riley 2019: 30–33). This was a system that John Knight was intimately familiar with, having used canals for a similar purpose on his farms at Lea Castle (Pitt 1810: 95–6). Similarly, both canals were dug to accommodate the 'tub-boats' that were commonly used in North Devon and Cornwall (Harris and Ellis 1972). However, the project was never completed, with the canals remaining unconnected and the railway tracks dismantled prior to 1835, possibly because John Knight was unable to secure support from neighbouring landowners, whose estates would have been traversed by the railway (SHC DD/BR/bn/31). As with many early schemes, the realisation that 'high' farming was unsustainable on The Chains probably forced John Knight to reconsider his original plans.

Without a reliable and vast source of income, it was impossible to maintain the frantic pace of improvement witnessed during the initial decade. As surviving receipt bundles reveal, despite a decade of very expensive landscape-scale irrigation and drainage projects, by 1837, the estate was still incapable of growing enough feed to support its livestock and had failed to create sufficient pastures for year-round grazing. Instead, regular shipments of oats and hay were being purchased at a considerable expense to maintain John Knight's new herds of 'improved' livestock (SHC A/EJM/3/5/3 Receipts for February to March 1837). The failure to 'reclaim' the moorland and make Exmoor self-sufficient, let alone profitable, was compounded by an inability to secure an external source of funding for reclamation. Most notably, as the closest male descendant of the wealthy connoisseur Richard Payne Knight of Downton Castle, Herefordshire, John Knight had expected a major inheritance that would have supported his efforts on Exmoor. However, the Payne Knight estate was passed to a niece (Charlotte Rouse-Boughton), leading to a legal battle in Chancery that dragged on until 1840, when John Knight lost (Orwin and Sellick 1970: 29–31). With the Knights now solely reliant upon their iron works and a couple of mildly successful estates in the Midlands, many of the more ambitious plans for Exmoor were reconsidered or altered. In January 1835, John Knight even considered abandoning 'demesne-farming' and letting 6000 acres (2428 ha) on The Chains to businessmen 'who are inclined to form a company for sheep farming on Exmoor'. However, he soon changed his mind, concluding that 'Cornham Farm would be quite spoilt' by such an endeavour (SHC A/EJM/1/1/5 John Knight to Frederic Knight, 20 January 1835). Although the period between the late 1820s and early 1830s is poorly documented, after 1835, the surviving evidence indicates that the scope, speed, focus and intent of reclamation had changed dramatically.

Whereas the reclamation projects conducted between 1819 and 1821 were concentrated around a 'central band' that stretched west to east from Pinkery across Cornham, Simonsbath and Honeymead, those conducted between 1835 and 1843 were far more geographically disparate. Furthermore, during these years, the estate focused entirely on open-cut drains and the creation of pasture. According to the accounts for 1835–1836, while surface drains continued to be cut on The Chains, Cornham Close and the North Forest, they were also created in new areas, such as Sparcombe, Blackpitts, Duredon and Limecombe (SHC A/BAZ/1/8 Osmond Lock's Accounts 1835–1836). The 1839–1840 accounts record that these drains were further intensified and lengthened. Specifically, from July 1839 to November 1839, a single labourer, William Rawle, was paid to cut 1049 chains (21 km) of drainage at Prayway and build five culverts, whilst also 'scouring and making 936 chains + 1 perch of surface drains' (19 km) on the 'North Chains'. In April 1839, several drains were also repaired and extended on Hearliving, Little Aschombe and Trout Hill, which had all been sites of repeated drainage in the previous two decades. However, by the late 1830s and early 1840s, the geographic attention of the Knights had shifted from focusing solely on the 'central band' to include other areas of the estate. In the 'South Forest', a small number of drains were cut 'on the boundary of North Molton Common' in April and May 1839, 29 perches (146 m) on Duredon in July 1839, and 78 perches (392 m) of surface drains on the Warren. On the northern extremities of the estate, the area that would become Larkbarrow Farm makes its first appearance in the accounts in April 1839, with 80 chains (1.6 km) of drainage being created (SHC A/EJM/3/3/3 Osmond Lock's Accounts 1839–1840; A/EJM/3/3/4 John Litson's

Monthly Accounts 1840–1841). The disparate nature of these new drains suggests that John Knight had now abandoned his initial system of interlocking arable and pastoral fields on Exmoor.

In contrast to open-cut drainage, between 1835 and 1843, there were no records of undersoil drainage and only three new irrigation projects. In December 1835, 'floating gutters' were made on Ashcombe, and then a water-carriage was constructed on Duredon in December 1836 (SHC A/BAZ/1/8 Osmond Lock's Accounts 1835–1836). These were joined in February 1840 by a new system of water-carriages to create 'flush-irrigation' in the fields surrounding Cornham Farm (SHC A/EJM/3/3/4 John Litson's Monthly Accounts 1840–1841). This switch in focus suggests that by 1835, John Knight had dropped any plans for 'high' farming and was instead attempting to secure the estate's profitability through pastoral farming alone. Indeed, in the receipts for April 1837, there is evidence that existing water-carriages on Ashcombe were being converted to form 'the head channel of the drainage system' (SHC A/EJM/3/5/3 Receipt Bundle March-April 1837). Similarly, the only references to arable farming in the accounts are for lands that John Knight held outside the Royal Forest in the manor of Brendon (SHC A/EJM/3/5/1 Work Assignments May 1831). Consequently, the arguments from contemporaries that John Knight's 'failure' was due to his dogged persistence with arable farming in a 'climate that made corn-growing at any price unprofitable' are clearly inaccurate (Sidney 1878). According to the rediscovered accounts, between 1835 and 1843, John Knight attempted to pivot Exmoor from 'mixed' or 'high' farming towards a purely pastoral endeavour.

Unlike irrigation, infrastructure and drainage, the surviving accounts rarely provide precise data regarding the application of lime as an 'artificial fertiliser' on Exmoor. However, recent studies have shown that liming was a key driver of ecological change within peatland environments (Rowney et al. 2022, 2023). Certainly, throughout John Knight's tenure, heavy applications of lime were presented as the solution for 'valueless' acid-peat moorland. Prior to his arrival on Exmoor, agricultural writers had already noticed Knight's fondness for lime. On his estates in Worcestershire, approximately 'four tons per acre' were used, which even early nineteenth-century improvers regarded as 'a great expenditure' (Pitt 1810: 95–6). The struggle to improve vast swathes of Exmoor turned this reliance into an obsession. According to letters from his sons, John Knight's 'chief object' was securing a stable source of limestone. Following the failure of his planned railway and canal, which would have allowed the importation of artificial fertilisers, many expensive prospecting projects were begun to discover a 'native' source of lime (SHC A/BAZ/1/5 Charles Knight to Unknown, May 1840). When these schemes failed, Knight attempted to purchase the neighbouring quarry of Challacombe Lime Rock at an exorbitant rate to 'service hopes almost extinct of possessing the calcareous pineapple within the Ring Fence' (SHC A/EJM/1/1/3 John Knight to Frederic Knight, 2 March 1833). The likening of lime to a rare fruit reveals the importance placed upon it. Indeed, John Knight's accounts suggest that all his attempts to convert the moorland into pasture post-1835 necessitated an intensive course of liming. Throughout February 1839, for example, the fields surrounding Cornham Farm were covered with 'constant courses of lime' to prepare them for the arrival of a new herd of cattle (SHC A/EJM/3/3/5 Exmoor Receipts and Disbursements 1842–1843). This aligned with contemporary opinion, which argued that whenever wasteland was 'manured with lime, the artificial grasses generally thrive' (Billingsley 1807). As such, lime became a panacea for the 'unproductive' soils of Exmoor.

The chronological patterns of reclamation revealed by these accounts highlight John Knight's changing fortunes and the importance of his contributions. Of the 203 drainage and irrigation projects recorded in the estate accounts between 1818 and 1897, 106 were conducted prior to 1835. During the remainder of John Knight's management of Exmoor (1836–1842), a further 45 entries would be added, albeit six of these included cleaning, repairing or extending existing channels. In contrast, there were only 52 projects during the whole of Frederic Knight's tenure (1843–1897), including four schemes extending existing gutters and 12 entries dubiously entered by the estate's steward, Robert Smith, as reimbursement for work on his personal farmstead (Baker et al. 2023). The number and variety of projects enacted during the initial decades (1818–1835) reflect John Knight's sincere belief that Exmoor could support 'high farming', a personal hope that 'reclamation' could be sustained through the Payne Knight inheritance, and the exploitation of autocratic 'demesne-farming' to undertake vast projects without opposition. However, when both the family inheritance and 'latent fertility' of Exmoor failed to materialise, Knight was forced to reassess, converting some arable projects to pasture and scrapping others. In contrast, Frederic Knight's tenure was characterised by efforts to transfer expenditure and minimise outgoings via tenant farming and sheep ranching (French and Baker

2023). The issues with relying upon new tenants to conduct 'permanent improvements' will be detailed in Chapter "Frederic Knight and Robert Smith, 1843–1862", but current archaeological surveys indicate that tenants only made minor adjustments to pre-existing drainage systems. This was largely because the estate sought to place new farms close to the drainage projects initiated under John Knight (SHC A/EJM/3/3/7 Accounts Relating to Farm and Estate Buildings; Riley 2019: 41). Consequently, the improvement projects initiated under John Knight were not only the most extensive witnessed during the nineteenth century but also provided the foundations for the subsequent distribution of tenant farms, and the shape of Exmoor agriculture to the end of the century.

EXPERIENCING RECLAMATION: LABOURERS AND LIVESTOCK

The changing fortunes of reclamation under John Knight are similarly reflected in the animal population of Exmoor. During the initial years of his ownership, Knight allowed the practice of seasonal pasturage to continue, albeit only as a temporary private arrangement and not a continuation of former common rights (*TCWA*, 20 August 1818, 1 April 1819, 14 June 1820, 14 June 1821). In 1826, cattle were kept year-round on Exmoor by the Knight estate for the first time, and the practice of renting out the moor for seasonal pasturage was quietly terminated in 1831 (SHC A/BAZ/1/5 John Knight to Jane Knight, 12 October 1826; *NDJ*, 26 May 1831). In terms of stock, John Knight rejected traditional breeds of North Devon Ruby cattle and Exmoor Horned Sheep for the more fashionable Highland cattle and a mixture of Cheviot and Merino sheep (Orwin and Sellick 1970: 64–6). The choice of Highland cattle was certainly inspired by Knight's interest in Scottish agriculture, as he described the breed as the 'most beautiful of animals' and believed that they could 'survive the inclement weather' better than the native breeds (SHC A/BAZ/1/5 John Knight to Jane Knight, 12 October 1826). Equally, according to contemporary commentators, the Exmoor Horned Sheep was believed to be too wild and produced a wool that was 'too coarse' to sell for any profit and thus should be replaced with 'improved' stock (Wilson 1856). Cheviot and Merino sheep were also purchased from Scotland, where it was believed they had now 'acclimatised to the harsh conditions' (SHC A/EJM/1/1/6 Frederic Knight to Jane Knight, 28 June 1841). Consequently, as the estate shifted towards a pastoral focus during the 1830s, large purchases of stock were made. As Table 1

Table 1   Cow stock on Exmoor, 1829–1835

Year	Cows	Bulls	Calves/steers	Total	Bought from Falkirk
1829	59	–	27	86	–
1830	64	5	53	122	–
1831	207	18	55	280	150
1832	450	9	131	590	196
1833	539	29	288	856	248
1834	604	9	277	890	245
1835	749	14	434	1197	235

Source: SHC A/EJM/3/3/2, Exmoor Cow Stock Book

demonstrates, between 1829 and 1835, the herd of Highland cattle increased from 86 to 1197. This necessitated extensive buying from fairs in Scotland, most notably Falkirk. Unfortunately, there are no equivalent details of the size of the sheep flock, but it can be estimated from the yearly sales advertisements placed in local newspapers. In 1842, for example, 520 Scotch Cattle and 900 Cheviot and Merino sheep were advertised for sale (*TCWA*, 7 September 1842). This suggests that Knight's flock numbered in the low thousands. The following year, the sale yielded approximately £6000, making these herds the single largest source of 'native' income for the Knight family (*Bristol Mercury*, 30 September 1843). Although this was certainly impressive, highland cattle alone could not generate the sums needed to convert the moorland into permanent pasture.

Until recently, the identities and working conditions of those who conducted reclamation have been overlooked (Siraut 2009: 117–24). In terms of pay, labourers on Exmoor earnt between 10s and 12s per week, with managers, carpenters, craftsmen and blacksmiths being paid a maximum of 15s. This was higher than the regional average, with wages in North Devon and West Somerset varying between 6s to 9s per week (SHC A/EJM/3/3/4 John Litson's Monthly Accounts 1840–1841; Acland and Sturge 1851: 28–9). Yet, the surviving accounts suggest that despite this, the Knights struggled to secure a stable workforce. Between 1819 and 1821, a mixture of local men and trusted hands from Worcestershire completed the foundational projects. 'Exmoor Abstract No. 1' records payments for 'lodgings at Lynton' for men such 'Lavendar', 'Charles' and 'Patricks' whilst also the 'carriage fare' of 'Davies', 'Lovell' and 'Smith' from Exford and South Molton. Similarly, in January 1820, John Knight paid 7s to 'bring the dead body of King from the Chains to Simonsbath' and then £3 10s for a coffin and 'carrying the body to be buried at Wolverley'. During this initial period, John Knight also hired 'agricultural gangs' as the expenses include £2 9s 6d on 'Breakfast and Drink for Johnson's Gang' (SHC A/EJM/3/3/1 Exmoor Abstract No. 1, f. 20; Verdon 2001). In contrast, following the shift towards pastoral farming in the 1830s, most of the landscape-scale drainage projects were assigned to individual labourers who were given a few months to complete a project, as in the case of William Rawle in 1839, noted above. This shift may reflect the estate's financial woes, but repeated payments to a few men like Rawle also suggest that the estate struggled to retain labourers on Exmoor. The account books record the high turnover of estate managers and labourers. Between January 1839 and February 1840, Cornham Farm passed between three managers (Henry Baker, John Dallyn and Joseph Harris) and dozens of unnamed labourers. The tasks they were responsible for during this period included cutting 38 perches of surface drains on Great Cornham; the creation of 'Cornham New Field'; cutting 82 perches of water-carriage for irrigation; laying 53 perches of underground drains; building 165 chains of 'floating-gutters'; cutting 75 chains of surface drains surrounding Cornham; and the creation of a new catch-water-meadow (SHC A/EJM/3/3/3 Osmond Lock's Accounts 1839–1840). The strenuous nature of reclamation and the harsh environment ensured that high wages were not enough to keep labourers on Exmoor.

The transience of local workers is further supported by the census, which demonstrates the sharp decrease of the 'live-in' labour force on the moorland between 1819 and 1841. In 1821, the population of Royal Forest was 113, of whom 12 were women. By 1831, this had decreased to 52, who were all living in the new farms and cottages. The population then increased in 1841 to 167, including 47 women, but it has been esti-mated that another 100 men travelled into Exmoor each week. (NA HO 71/78 1831 Census; HO 107/965 1841 Census; Orwin and Sellick 1970: 61, 115). The fact that this gender imbalance was akin to a colonial settlement was not lost on John Knight. Commenting on the difficulty of acquiring a shepherd, he wrote:

> I am doing my best to fit up the White Rock Cottage for a family, but society I cannot provide; indeed several servants have lately left my station for want of company. (John Knight to Jane Knight, May 1828, Orwin and Sellick 1970: 66)

John Knight copied the Scottish Bothy system, in which large numbers of men were barracked in cottages, such as Hoar Oak or Cloven Rocks, situated close to areas undergoing 'improvement'. In one case, 11 labourers were recorded in a single-roomed cottage while the average occupancy was six men to a cottage (NA HO 71/78 1831 Census; HO 107/965 1841 Census). Similarly, the inventories for 1829 reveal that there were 22 'men's blankets' stored at the Warren cottages and 22 more at Cornham Farm, indicating that occupancy rates could be even higher (SHC A/BAZ/1/6 Inventory of Land, Stock & Contents of Properties). Furthermore, cutting open drains or water-carriages during this period was dangerous and difficult. In 1844, for example, an inquest found that William Crochford was 'digging a drain in a meadow, about six feet deep and five feet wide' on Exmoor when the 'boggy soil' collapsed. He was 'found in a dying state, buried up to his chin'. Although the jury returned a verdict of Accidental Death, it was noted that Crochford had been sent to complete his task 'entirely alone' (*TCWA*, 24 January 1844). The difficulties of transporting large machinery and animal teams to the isolated moorlands meant that most work had to be conducted by hand. The inventories for 1829–1833, for instance, reveal that the estate retained numerous 'breast ploughs for subsoil draining' but only two animal-drawn variants (SHC A/BAZ/1/6 Inventory of Land, Stock & Contents of Properties). Consequently, the combination of isolation, dangerous working conditions and poor living conditions ensured that by the 1840s, the Knights relied upon a small cadre of permanent staff supplemented by local labourers who were called in when needed for large projects.

By the 1830s, many of these 'permanent staff' were Irish workers hired from his father-in-law's estate in County Kerry to run peat-fired lime kilns and conduct drainage. A letter from Lord Headley dated 1839 details a system of 'headhunting' that was already well established:

Darby, poor Peter's brother, was here the other day to look out for another three Labourers for your Father to take over to the Forest, who were accustomed to burn Lime in Running Kilns … he got three Men from this Neighbourhood, able bodied men, who would do well if they go, and with those already in the Forest from Ireland, would be able to do all that is wanting in this line at first, that is to cut turf and saw in Summer and burn Lime in Winter (SHC A/BAZ/1/5 Lord Headley to Frederic Knight, 14 April 1839)

Irish labourers were preferred not merely to keep wages low or avoid employing local men and women who might still resent enclosure but also because Knight believed that they understood the 'soils' of Exmoor better than any labourer from Somerset or Devon. In 1840, he commented on an Irishman hired the previous year, stating: 'He is quite different from the wild race I employ here ... ignorant as they are of sheep, and [the land] liable to the mismanagement of the native' (SHC A/BAZ/1/5 John Knight to Unknown, n.d. 1840). As Corrine Fowler has noted, by the nineteenth century, Irish people had become intimately associated with the moors of Britain (Fowler 2020). By 1842, the accounts reveal that there were 22 'Irishmen' employed year-round, compared to between 26 and 48 other workers (grooms, carpenters, blacksmiths, shepherds, herds-men, ploughmen, levellers, gardeners, labourers, carters and keepers) whose numbers varied monthly (SHC A/EJM/3/3/4 John Litson's Monthly Accounts 1840–1841). As John Knight acknowledged, by this period, their role had expanded beyond agriculture and that he had now 'formed a guard of young Irishmen for my protection and [I will] call them gamekeepers' (SHC A/BAZ/1/5 John Knight to Frederic Knight 28 July 1841). Armed with what one newspaper described as 'formidable looking shillelaghs', they were used to combat poaching and sheep steal-ing on Exmoor (*Western Courier*, 23 September 1840). Despite their ser-vice, John Knight shared contemporary prejudices about his Irish workers, writing: 'Irish labourers—I find these Potatoe [sic] eaters must all come from the same part of Ireland or they would do nothing but fight' (SHC A/BAZ/1/5 John Knight to Unknown, Draft Letter, 16 August 1841).

The formation of a 'guard' of Irishmen reveals that the relationship between the Knights and the local population remained fractious. As in many rural communities across Britain, enclosure was met by local resis-tance. However, due to Exmoor's tiny, dispersed population, this came not in the form of the 'traditional' enclosure riot but took subtler forms, such as trespass, that are difficult to uncover in the historical record, which frustrates an accurate assessment of the breadth or character of resistance during this period (McDonagh 2013; Blomley 2007; Winchester 2022). For example, throughout the 1820s and early 1830s, John Knight repeat-edly issued warnings regarding trespassing animals. According to one of his lawyers, the common practice used by locals to circumvent the new legal and material enclosure of Exmoor was that 'they have only to feed their sheep upon the adjoining commons and they will [then] eat up your pasture without paying any thing for it' (SHC A/EJM/1/3/1 Richard

Strong to John Knight, 13 January 1819). Similarly, in the 1830s, newspaper reports reveal that John Knight joined a prosecution society to protect Exmoor landowners from poachers, trespassers and unlicensed fishermen. This offered a reward of 'one guinea' for any information 'as shall lead to the conviction of any one poaching with nets' (*Dorset County Chronicle*, 5 March 1835). Such actions suggest that there is some form of 'everyday resistance' towards the initial enclosure of Exmoor (Neeson 1993).

These acts of 'social crime' or 'everyday resistance' were reinforced by a couple of major incidents. Most significantly, in 1834, an unknown assailant climbed up to the window of John Knight's steward, Osmond Lock, and fired a pistol into his bed. Although the shot missed, John Knight informed the Home Office that the perpetrator was probably 'one of the agricultural labourers' who was 'aggrieved by the current distressed state of the region' (NA HO/64/4/38, ff. 93–98 John Knight to the Home Office, 4 March 1834, 12 March 1834). Previously, Knight illustrated the extent of local hostility to Lock, by reporting in passing that 'the labourers have been stealing the potatoes; beating Lock etc: for all which I shall be amply a match for them' (A/EJM/1/1/5 John Knight to Frederic Knight, 20 January 1835). Indeed, nobody in the local community provided any information about the attempted shooting despite a £100 reward and a pardon for any accomplices (*Morning Chronicle*, 19 March 1834). As such, it appears that this act of attempted murder was the culmination of growing resentment within the local community. Similarly, in 1844, 'part of the farm' at Brendon Barton was burnt down by suspected incendiaries. The then steward, John Mogridge, sent 'two parties' of the estate's gamekeepers and bailiffs to 'investigate the circumstance' and question locals. Unable to find a culprit, Mogridge speculated that it was probably the work of those aggrieved by John Knight's efforts to prevent them 'repeatedly setting fire to different parts of Brendon Common'. As Mogridge wrote to Frederic Knight:

> My opinion is if you were not to interfere you would not have so much of the common burnt as at present ... And after all it is impossible to prevent its being done with the will of the parties having been set so against you ... and if we were to attack them I fear the reward would be same of course. (SHC A/EJM/1/1/7 John Mogridge to Frederic Knight, 10 Mary 1844)

As noted previously, Knight's desire to create his own personal fiefdom on Exmoor disrupted many of the established customs and social relationships within the region. In response, acts of protest served as a momentary rebuke from a local population who had been repeatedly denigrated and dispossessed.

CONCLUSION: UNDERESTIMATING JOHN KNIGHT

Eventually, a combination of financial and personal difficulties ensured that even the slower-paced reclamation witnessed post-1835 would cease. By 1837, Jane Knight was no longer able to live at Simonsbath due to ill health and so John Knight left Exmoor for Jersey. Knight was now in his 70s, and confided to his family now that 'My locomotive powers are so fallen off', travel around the estate was difficult. However, he still hoped that his sons, Frederic and Charles Knight, 'will pay attention to the economy of the [Exmoor] business and that it will then be a most profitable concern' (SHC A/BAZ/1/5 John Knight to Frederic Knight, 10 February 1838). However, this did not seem to be likely in the short-term, and in one of their final letters, Frederic Knight asked his father to 'endeavour to live as long as you possibly can, as your death before the affairs of the forest are more settled would be the greatest calamity that could befall the family' (SHC A/EJM/1/1/6 Frederic Knight to John Knight, 7 March 1849). Eventually, Jane and John Knight opted for the better climate of Rome in 1839, and both died in Italy, despite frequently expressing their desire to return (SHC A/EJM/1/1/6 Frederic Knight to Jane Knight, 19 March 1841, Frederic Knight to John Knight 22 September 1843, Frederic Knight to John Knight, 9 December 1845). Although John Knight remained very engaged with his son's 'improvement' projects, the loss of the Payne Knight inheritance in 1840 seems to have extinguished his optimistic vision of the complete reclamation of Exmoor. Indeed, it was not only John Knight who found his confidence in the reclamation of Exmoor shaken during the 1840s. By this period, anonymous newspaper correspondents were criticising the 'demesne-farming' plan, claiming that if Knight had:

> erected about fifty farm houses with offices, and enclosed about two or three hundred acres of land round the same, on some of the dry hills, and let the same at a low rent for long terms of years, the forest at this period would

have brought him in at least *double the income it now does*, it would have encouraged industry, and prevented a vast number of agriculturists from emigrating to America and other foreign parts. (*Western Courier*, 17 October 1840)

These criticisms turned discourses of internal colonialism against John Knight, and depicted his plans for reclamation as wasteful and unindustrious. Despite overseeing decades of intensive reclamation projects that would provide the foundations for all future improvement, by the mid-nineteenth century, the popular perception of John Knight's tenure was that he had treated Exmoor as 'merely a large plaything' (SHC A/EJM/1/1/3 Frederic Knight to Ann Headley, 12 December 1851). Such claims contain a kernel of truth, because John Knight did reject traditional but profitable sheep farming in favour of an overly ambitious mixed farming scheme, based on unfinished transport infrastructure, and dependent on a doubtful family inheritance. Yet, over time, the belief that John Knight's approach to reclamation was ill-planned, abortive and reckless would obfuscate and misattribute some of the most significant, and carefully thought out, drainage, irrigation and infrastructure projects ever witnessed in England.

REFERENCES

SOMERSET HERITAGE CENTRE

A/BAZ/1/5, Charles Knight to Unknown, May 1840.
A/BAZ/1/5, John Knight to Charles Knight, 30 December 1841.
A/BAZ/1/5, John Knight to Frederic Knight, 10 February 1838.
A/BAZ/1/5, John Knight to Frederic Knight, 28 July 1841.
A/BAZ/1/5, John Knight to Jane Knight, August 1826.
A/BAZ/1/5, John Knight to Jane Knight, 12 October 1826.
A/BAZ/1/5, John Knight to Unknown, n.d. 1840.
A/BAZ/1/5, John Knight to Unknown, Draft Letter, 16 August 1841.
A/BAZ/1/5, Lord Headley to Frederic Knight, 14 April 1839.
A/BAZ/1/6, Inventory of Land, Stock and Contents of Properties on Exmoor.
A/BAZ/1/8, Osmond Lock's Accounts, 1835–1836.
A/EJM/1/1/3, Frederic Knight to Ann Headley, 12 December 1851.
A/EJM/1/1/3, John Knight to Frederic Knight, 2 March 1833.
A/EJM/1/1/5, John Knight to Frederic Knight, 20 January 1835.
A/EJM/1/1/6, Frederic Knight to Jane Knight, 19 March 1841.

A/EJM/1/1/6, Frederic Knight to John Knight, 22 September 1843.
A/EJM/1/1/6, Frederic Knight to John Knight, 9 December 1845.
A/EJM/1/1/6, Frederic Knight to John Knight, 7 March 1849.
A/EJM/1/1/6, Frederic Knight to John Knight, 6 January 1850.
A/EJM/1/1/7, John Mogridge to Frederic Knight, 10 May 1844.
A/EJM/1/3/1, Richard Strong to John Knight, 13 January 1819.
A/EJM/1/3/1, Richard Strong to John Knight, 21 March 1819.
A/EJM/1/3/2, George Allanson-Winn to John Knight, 7 June 1821.
A/EJM/3/3/1, Exmoor Abstract No. 1.
A/EJM/3/3/2, Exmoor Cow Stock Book.
A/EJM/3/3/3, Osmond Lock's Accounts, 1839–1840.
A/EJM/3/3/4, John Litson's Monthly Accounts, 1840–1841.
A/EJM/3/3/5, Exmoor Receipts and Disbursements, 1842–1843.
A/EJM/3/3/7, Accounts Relating to Farm and Estate Buildings on Exmoor.
A/EJM/3/5/1, Work Assignments May 1831.
A/EJM/3/5/3, Receipts for February–March 1837.
A/EJM/3/5/3, Receipts for March–April 1837.
DD/BR/bn/31 John Knight to Charles Bailey, Nynehead, railroad from Porlock, 1826–1827

THE NATIONAL ARCHIVES (UK)

CRES/2/1503, Exmoor Inclosure Reports, Office of Woods, Forests and Land Revenues.
HO/64/4/38, John Knight, Simonsbath, to the Home Office, 4 March 1834, Home Office Disturbance Papers, ff. 93–94.
HO/64/4/38, John Knight, Simonsbath, to the Home Office, 12 March 1834, Home Office Disturbance Papers, ff. 95–98.
HO 71/78 1831 Census, Home Office Records.
HO 107/965, 1841 Census, Home Office Records.
LR/5/1/2, Accounts of William Lock Deputy Forester, Office of the Auditors of Land Revenue.

NEWSPAPERS

Bath Chronicle, 14 October 1819.
Bristol Mercury, 30 September 1843.
Exeter Flying Post, 20 August 1873.
Devizes & Wiltshire Gazette, 11 January 1844.
Dorset County Chronicle, 5 March 1835, 18 June 1835.
Dundee Courier, 5 March 1844.
Illustrated London News 22 October 1853.

Kerry Examiner, 20 August 1841.
London Evening Standard, 7 August 1867.
Morning Chronicle, 19 March 1834, 10 August 1849.
Morning Post, 10 August 1863.
Norfolk News, 14 February 1846.
North Devon Journal, 26 May 1831, 9 November 1843, 8 September 1853, 4 October 1860, 4 October 1863.
Public Ledger & Daily Advertiser, 28 December 1833.
Sun, 10 June 1835.
Taunton Courier, 20 August 1818, 22 October 1818, 29 October 1818, 1 April 1819, 14 June 1820, 14 June 1821, 15 April 1829, 7 September 1842, 24 January 1844
West Briton & Cornwall Advertiser, 24 July 1818.
Western Times, 10 July 1847.
Western Courier, 23 September 1840, 17 October 1840.
Wolverhampton Chronicle, 26 December 1832.

PRIMARY PRINTED SOURCES

Acland, T., and W. Sturge. 1851. *The Farming of Somersetshire*. London: John Murray.
Billingsley, J. 1798. *General View of the Agricultural of Somerset, with Observations on the Means of its Improvement*. Bath: R. Cruttwell.
———. 1807. An Essay on the Best Methods of Inclosing, Dividing and Cultivating Waste Lands. *Letters and Papers on Agriculture, Planting &c. Addressed to the Society Instituted at Bath* 11: 1–93.
Darby, J. 1873. The Farming of Somerset. *Journal of the Bath and West of England Society* 5: 96–172.
England in 1830: Being a Letter to (the Late) Earl Grey, Laying Before Him the Condition of the People as Described by Themselves in their Petitions to Parliament. 1831. London.
Pusey, P. 1853. On the Agricultural Improvements of Lincolnshire. *Journal of the Royal Agricultural Society of England* 4: 287–315.
King, A. 1884. Exmoor and its People. *Argosy* 38: 301.
Lock, P. 1746/1792. *An Exmoor Scolding, in the Propriety and Decency of Exmoor Language, Also, An Exmoor Courtship. Together with Notes, and a Vocabulary For Explaining Uncouth Expressions, and Interpreting Barbarous Words and Phrases*. Exeter: Thorn & Son.
Locke J. 1988. *Two Treatise of Government*. Edited by P. Laslett. Cambridge: Cambridge University Press.
Pitt, W. 1810. *General View of the Agriculture of the County of Worcester, with Observations on the Means of its Improvement*. London: R. Phillips.

Sidney, S. 1878. Exmoor Reclamation. *Journal of the Royal Agricultural Society of England* 2 (14): 72–97.

Snell, F.J. 1903. *The Book of Exmoor*. London: Halsgrove.

Spender, E., and T.W.P. Isaac. 1858. The Labourer. *Journal of the Bath and West of England Society* 6: 130–177.

Wagstaffe, J. 1805. On Reclaiming Waste Lands. *Letters and Papers on Agriculture, Planting &c... Bath and West of England Society* 10: 18–22.

Wilson, J. 1856. On the Various Breeds of Sheep in Great Britain, Especially with Reference to the Character and Value of their Wool. *Journal of the Royal Agricultural Society of England*. 16: 222–248.

SECONDARY WORKS

Arneil, B. 2012. Liberal Colonialism, Domestic Colonies and Citizenship. *History of Political Thought* 33 (3): 491–523. https://www.jstor.org/stable/26225797.

———. 2017. *Domestic Colonies: The Turn Inward to Colony*. Oxford: Oxford University Press. https://doi.org/10.1093/oso/9780198803423.001.0001.

———. 2019. The Failure of Planned Happiness: The Rise and Fall of British Home Colonies. In *Happiness and Utility: Essays Presented to Frederic Rosen*, ed. G. Varouxakis and M. Philp, 269–288. London: UCL Press. https://doi.org/10.2307/j.ctvf3w1s5.18.

———. 2020. Origins: Colonies and Statistics. *Canadian Journal of Political Science* 53 (4): 735–754. https://doi.org/10.1017/S000842392000116X.

Atkins, W. 2014. *The Moor: Lives, Landscape, Literature*. London: Faber & Faber.

Baker, L., F. Rowney, H. French, and R. Fyfe. 2023. Revolution and Continuity? Reassessing Nineteenth-Century Moorland Reclamation Through Palaeoecological and Historical Research. *Landscape Research* 49: 48–63. https://doi.org/10.1080/01426397.2023.2244904.

Bhandar, B. 2018. *Colonial Lives of Property: Law, Land, and the Racial Regimes of Ownership*. Durham NC: Duke University Press. https://doi.org/10.2307/j.ctv11smjpm.

Blomley, N. 2007. Making Private Property: Enclosure, Common Right and the Work of Hedges. *Rural History*. 18 (1): 1–21. https://doi.org/10.1017/S0956793306001993.

Bull, P. 2010. Irish Land and British Politics. In *The Land Question in Britain, 1750–1950*, ed. M. Cragoe and P. Readman, 126. Basingstoke: Palgrave Macmillan. https://doi.org/10.1057/9780230248472.

Burton, R.A. 1989. *The Heritage of Exmoor*. Maslands Ltd.

Cook, H., and T. Williamson. 2007. In *'The Later History of Water-Meadows' in Water Meadows: History, Ecology and Conservation*, ed. H. Cook and T. Williamson, 52–69. Macclesfield: Windgather Press.

Cragoe, M. 2010. "A Contemptible Mimic of the Irish": The Land Question in Victorian Wales. In *The Land Question in Britain, 1750–1950*, ed. M. Cragoe and P. Readman, 92–108. Basingstoke: Palgrave Macmillan. https://doi.org/10.1057/9780230248472.

Eastwood, D. 1997. *Government and Community in the English Provinces, 1700–1870*. London: Palgrave Macmillan. https://doi.org/10.1007/978-1-349-25673-0.

Fitzpatrick, R. 2018. The Demesne Farm at Inch, 1738–56. *Irish Economic and Social History* 45: 115–135. https://www.jstor.org/stable/26739504.

Fowler, C. 2020. *Green Unpleasant Land: Creative Responses to Rural England's Colonial Connections*. London: Peepal Tree. https://search.ebscohost.com/login.aspx?direct=true&db=nlebk&AN=2899715&site=ehost-live.

Fox, H.S.A. 1991. 'Farming Practice and Techniques: Devon and Cornwall. In *The Agrarian History of England and Wales: Volume III, 1348–1500*, ed. E. Miller, 303–323. Cambridge: Cambridge University Press.

Fussell, G.E. 1948. "High Farming" in Southwestern England, 1840–1880. *Economic Geography* 24 (1): 53–73. https://doi.org/10.2307/141039.

French, H., and L. Baker. 2023. "The result never quite equalled the promise": Risk, Reward and Reclamation on Exmoor, 1840–1897. *Agricultural History Review*. 71 (1): 45–65.

Gillard M. 2002. The Medieval Landscape of the Exmoor Region: Enclosure and Settlement in an Upland Fringe. Unpublished PhD Thesis, University of Exeter.

Griffin, C. 2020. *The Politics of Hunger: Protest, Poverty and Policy in England, c. 1750–c.1840*. Manchester: Manchester University Press. http://www.jstor.org/stable/j.ctvx078dt.

———. 2023. Enclosure as Internal Colonisation: The Subaltern Commoner, Terra Nullius and the Settling of England's "Wastes". *Transactions of the Royal Historical Society* 33: 95–120. https://doi.org/10.1017/S0080440123000014.

Hardyment, C. 2012. *Writing Britain: Wastelands to Wonderlands*. London: British Library Publishing.

Harris, C. 2004. How Did Colonialism Dispossess? Comments from an Edge of Empire. *Annals of the Association of American Geographers* 94 (1): 165–182. https://www.jstor.org/stable/3694073.

Harris, H., and M. Ellis. 1972. *The Bude Canal*. Newton Abbot: David & Charles.

Irvine, R. 2015. East Anglian Fenland: Water, the Work of Imagination and the Creation of Value. In *Waterworlds: Anthropology in Fluid Environments*, ed. K. Hastrup and F. Hastrup, 23–45. Bergahn. https://doi.org/10.1515/9781782389477.

Legacies of British Slavery Database. n.d. Robert Cunyingham of Braidland and Craig. Retrieved June 6, 2024, from http://wwwdepts-live.ucl.ac.uk/lbs/person/view/2146662369.

Lucey, D. Seán. 2011. *Land, Popular Politics and Agrarian Violence in Ireland: The Case of County Kerry, 1872–1886.* Dublin: University College Dublin Press.

MacDermot, E. 1973. *A History of the Forest of Exmoor.* Newton Abbot: David & Charles.

MacMahon, B. 2017. *The Great Famine in Tralee and North Kerry.* Cork: Mercier Press.

McDonagh, B. 2013. Making and Breaking Property: Negotiating Enclosure and Common Rights in Sixteenth-Century England. *History Workshop Journal.* 76: 32–56. http://www.jstor.org/stable/43298731.

Mingay, G.E. 1997. *Parliamentary Enclosure in England: An Introduction to its Causes, Incidence and Impact, 1750–1850.* London: Routledge.

Montaño, J. Patrick. 2011. *The Roots of English Colonialism in Ireland.* Cambridge: Cambridge University Press. https://doi.org/10.1017/CBO9780511996313.

Neeson, J. 1993. *Commoners: Common Right, Enclosure and Social Change in England.* Cambridge: Cambridge University Press. https://doi.org/10.1017/CBO9780511522741.

Neocleous, M. 2012. International Law as Primitive Accumulation; Or, the Secret of Systematic Colonization. *European Journal of International Law* 23 (4): 941–962. https://doi.org/10.1093/ejil/chs068.

O'Donell, R. 2015. *Assembling Enclosure: Transformations in the Rural Landscape of Post-Medieval North-East England.* Hatfield: University of Hertfordshire Press. https://ebookcentral.proquest.com/lib/exeter/detail.action?docID=4306681.

Orwin, C.S., and R.J. Sellick. 1970. *The Reclamation of Exmoor Forest.* Newton Abbot: David & Charles.

Poole, R. 2019. *Peterloo: The English Uprising.* Oxford: Oxford University Press. https://ebookcentral.proquest.com/lib/exeter/detail.action?docID=5824667.

Riley, H. 2019. *The Landscape of the Knights on Exmoor: A Case Study for the Exmoor Mires Partnership.* Dulverton: Exmoor Mires Projects. https://doi.org/10.5284/1082836.

Robinson, M. 1986. The Extent of Farm Underdrainage in England and Wales, prior to 1919. *Agricultural History Review* 34 (1): 79–85. https://www.jstor.org/stable/40274438.

Rowney, F., R. Fyfe, P. Anderson, R. Barnett, W. Blake, T. Daley, K. Head, A. Macleod, I. Matthews, and D. Smith. 2022. Ecological Consequences of Historic Moorland "Improvement". *Biodiversity and Conservation.* 31: 3131–3161. https://doi.org/10.1007/s10531-022-02479-6.

Rowney, F., R. Fyfe, L. Baker, H. French, H. Ombashi, R. Timms, M. Hall, and G. Milward. 2023. Historic Anthropogenic Disturbances Explain Long-Term Moorland Vegetation Dynamics. *Ecology and Evolution.* 13 (3): 1–17. https://doi.org/10.1002/ece3.9876.

Siraut, M. 2009. *Exmoor: The Making of an English Upland*. Chichester: Phillimore & Co.

Stone, D. 2005. *Decision-Making in Medieval Agriculture*. Oxford: Oxford University Press. https://doi.org/10.1093/acprof:oso/9780199247769.001.0001.

Turner, J. 2018. Internal Colonisation: The Intimate Circulations of Empire, Race and Liberal Government. *European Journal of International Relations* 24 (4): 765–790. https://doi.org/10.1177/1354066117734904.

Turner, M. 1980. *English Parliamentary Enclosure: Its Historical Geography and Economic History*. Folkestone: Dawson.

Verdon, N. 2001. The Employment of Women and Children in Agriculture: A Reassessment of Agricultural Gangs in Nineteenth-Century Norfolk. *Agricultural History Review*. 49 (1): 41–55. https://www.jstor.org/stable/40275688.

Winchester, A.J.L. 2022. *Common Land in Britain: A History from the Middle Ages to the Present Day*. Woodbridge: Boydell. https://doi.org/10.2307/j.ctv2f1smcz.

Frederic Knight and Robert Smith, 1843–1862

Abstract After John Knight's departure from Exmoor, his son Frederic divided the estate and built a series of farmhouses in the 1840s. From 1848 he employed a dynamic new estate steward, Lincolnshire agriculturalist, Robert Smith. This chapter shows how Smith shared the 'colonising' view of Exmoor, and applied it explicitly through a policy of attracting Midlands and Yorkshire farmers and ignoring local people, livestock and methods. Tenants were expected to fund estate improvements themselves, and their leases set demanding targets, which most found impossible to meet. Although Smith applied all these methods to his 'show-farm' of Emmett's Grange, even he struggled financially. Smith tried to compensate for the failure of the first generation of tenants by finding iron ore on the estate. When this failed too, his relationship with Frederic Knight broke down irretrievably.

Keywords Agrarian history • Social history • Nineteenth-century Britain • Colonial ideology • Domestic colonies • Moorlands • Development • Agrarian capitalism • Risk

H. French et al., *The Reclamation of Exmoor Revisited*,
https://doi.org/10.1007/978-3-031-81658-1_3

FINANCIAL PROBLEMS AND THE CREATION
OF TENANT FARMS

Following John Knight's departure in 1839, the Exmoor estate became the responsibility of his eldest son, Frederic Knight (Image 1). Although he was initially assisted by his brother, Charles, by 1843, Frederic Knight had become the unwilling sole manager of the former Royal Forest (SHC A/BAZ/1/5 Charles Knight to Frederic Knight, 23 October 1841).

Image 1 Photograph of Frederick Knight by Camille Silvy, 1860. (Source: National Portrait Gallery NPG Ax50359)

Critically, in 1841, Frederic Knight was elected as Tory MP for West Worcestershire, a seat he would hold until 1885. Although his only prominent government position was as Secretary to the Poor Law Board under Lord Derby (1858–1859), his parliamentary career was often at odds with his new duties on Exmoor. As he complained to his mother in 1841:

> I were a Farmer? Deuced disagreeable—go into Parliament? Uncommon, stupid—and yet, fate is fate and the man who was born & c—So then in the first place, how shall I get the power of doing any good on Exmoor? (SHC A/EJM/1/1/6 Frederic Knight to Jane Knight, 19 March 1841; Orwin and Sellick 1970: 36–38)

Frederic's original plan was to continue 'demesne-farming' at a reduced level, while letting a couple of farms:

> My proposal (in case Downton is lost) is to sell at Michaelmas the whole stock on the forest and discharge every man and to let Simonsbath and Cornham Farm … On the rest of the land, i.e. the South Forest, Warren, North Moor, and Badgeworthy, I shall take in stock to summer … (SHC A/EJM/1/1/6 Frederic Knight to John Knight, 25 June 1843)

However, financial difficulties and the failure to secure the Payne Knight inheritance soon made these plans impossible. Frederick became an absentee landlord and placed the day-to-day operation of Exmoor in the hands of a land agent, while he divided his time between his Parliamentary constituency, Wolverley, and London. While this arrangement resembles his Headley in-laws' management of their Irish estate, such non-residence was commonplace in southwest England, particularly in isolated or woodland communities, which were rarely visited by their landlord (Beardmore 2020). In fact, Knight's preference for politics (and Wolverley) was bound up with his effort to secure his father's inheritance of the Downton estate, to unlock the funds necessary for their grand plans for improvement. Frederick wrote to his father in 1841 'So much for Exmoor—now for Downton—the man who judged our case is a scoundrel, leader of the Whig party in Herefordshire, and our opponents great friend', who he could oppose in Parliament (SHC A/EJM/1/1/6 Frederic Knight to Jane Knight, 19 March 1841).

Local commentators were undismayed by Frederic Knight's departure. In fact, they praised his move as an improvement on his father's direct administration. The writer of a letter criticising John Knight's practice of 'demesne-farming' in *Western Courier* concluded: 'I should be pleased to see a good English farmer as Mr Knight's leading man' (*Western Courier*, 17 October 1840). Similarly, the *Exeter & Plymouth Gazette* praised Frederic Knight for placing the estate in the hands of a steward and 'endeavouring gradually to bring it more into the position of ordinary landed property' (*Exeter and Plymouth Gazette*, 18 Jan 1851). Unfortunately, little evidence survives to indicate what the locals, tenant farmers or land agents thought of Frederic Knight's departure. In March 1844, his desire to return to Exmoor to oversee the ongoing farm building work received a curt response from his new steward, John Mogridge of Molland, 'I do not see any necessity of you being here at present, in our present situation I think you are best away' (SHC A/EJM/1/1/7 John Mogridge to Frederic Knight, 24 March 1844). However, this arrangement did not last for long, and by June of that year, Mogridge wrote to Knight in terms that anticipated Robert Smith's later travails, complaining:

> I am vexed, more than vexed, that I cannot hear from you, and do think you ought to have sufficient confidence to put me in direct and immediate communication with you wherever you may happen to be ... There are things that I know you must be anxious about therefore it appears the more exhausting that I do not hear from you, having written more than once of the subject. (SHC A/EJM/1/1/7 John Mogridge to Frederic Knight, 26 June 1844)

Further complaints followed from Mogridge in January 1846, indicating that Knight's behaviour was ingrained (SHC A/EJM/1/1/7 John Mogridge to Frederic Knight, 22 January 1846). It also annoyed certain tenants, especially those in financial difficulties. In September 1851, Robert Smith reported that George Allen Harrold of Warren Farm had departed, feeling that he was being disrespected and ignored by his new landlord (SHC A/EJM/1/3/6 Robert Smith to Frederic Knight, 13 September 1851). However, although Frederic Knight was detached from the day-to-day farming of Exmoor, he still attempted to play the role of a considerate landowner. Smith's correspondence reveals that until the late 1850s, Knight tried to attend every Rent Day, meeting each of the tenants and hosting a dinner for them (SHC A/EJM/1/3/7 Robert Smith to Frederic Knight, 19 February 1852; A/EJM/1/3/8 Robert Smith to

Frederic Knight, 4 January 1853; A/EJM/1/3/10 Robert Smith to Frederic Knight, 25 January 1856). While this may reflect a certain distrust about Smith's financial management, it also suggests serious efforts to maintain a healthy relationship between tenant and landlord (SHC A/EJM/1/3/15 Robert Smith to Frederic Knight, 9 March 1859).

By 1847, Frederic Knight was spending £7200 more than his annual income and was facing repayment of the £50,000 mortgage used to purchase Exmoor (SHC A/EJM/1/1/6 Frederic Knight to John Knight, 28 January 1848). Moreover, the family's traditional sources of income had declined. Rents for Worcestershire, Bromsgrove and Exmoor brought in £4000 while 'the whole of the iron works' in Wolverley earnt only £3385 (SHC A/EJM/1/1/6 Rough Accounts, 29 May 1847). To prevent bankruptcy, Frederic was forced to sell the Bromsgrove estate. Although it sold for less than expected, enough capital was raised to placate their lenders and allow him to remake Exmoor (Orwin and Sellick 1970: 80; SHC A/EJM/1/1/6 Frederic Knight to John Knight, 13 September 1847; SHC A/EJM/2/5/1-5 Papers Relating to Bromsgrove & Stoke Prior, Worcs., c. 1850s). The decision to sell Bromsgrove rather than abandon Exmoor reveals the family's continuing belief that the moorland could be transformed into their primary asset.

The family's financial crisis convinced Frederic Knight that a new approach was needed. In 1847, he abandoned cattle farming, which had dominated John Knight's regime. As he explained to his father:

> Keeping a large lot of growing stock of different ages and allowing them to lose all the condition from 'bad keep', during the winter, that they have acquired in the Summer cannot pay. Now I believe that sheep summer fed on the Forest, put on turnips, and sold off late before Xmas would do so.
> (SHC A/EJM/1/1/6 Frederic Knight to John Knight, 13 September 1847)

Frederic held a series of sales, which disposed of the Highland cattle, Cheviot and Merino sheep (*Dorset County Chronicle*, 11 September 1845, 21 September 1847), and marked the final demise of John Knight's scheme of 'demesne-farming'. For the next 20 years, the estate's direct farming operations were minimal. It did not hold any stock on the moorland, or keep any agricultural land 'in-hand' for extended periods. Instead, Frederic hoped that all future cultivation, improvement and reclamation would be achieved by a new cadre of tenant farmers (SHC A/EJM/1/1/6 Frederic Knight to John Knight, 25 June 1843). After 1844, he divided the estate into a series of individual holdings and began an intensive period of farm building. This was managed by a new steward, John Mogridge, who oversaw the construction, conversion or improvement of 15 farmsteads (Orwin and Sellick 1970, 80–1). Invariably, these farms were built in areas where John Knight had already conducted drainage or irrigation work, particularly the 'central band' of Exmoor, where Frederic constructed Pinkery Farm, Driver (Dryford) Farm, Duredon (Duredown) Farm, Simonsbath Barton Farm, Gallon House (Red Deer) Farm and Inn, Winstitchen, Titchcombe and the Warren Farm (Riley 2019: 38–9). In addition, Simonsbath House was converted into a farmstead, after Frederic Knight became an absentee landlord. On Long Holcombe and the South Forest, Wintershead, Emmett's Grange, Horsen and Picked Stones farms were built. These would be the central focus during Robert Smith's tenure as steward, because he lived at Emmett's Grange and the more sheltered, south-facing location of these farms made them popular with incoming tenants. In contrast, Larkbarrow and Tom's Hill farms on the 'North Side' of the Forest were the most isolated on the estate and often lay empty for multiple years (SHC A/EJM/3/3/7 Farms and Estate Building Accounts, c. 1850s; SHC A/EJM/1/3/5 Financial Statements and Accounts for Exmoor, c. 1848–1857; SHC A/EJM/1/3/13 Robert Smith to Frederic Knight, 2 December 1857). Altogether, Frederic Knight spent £16,800 on new buildings, roads and fences during the mid-1840s, providing the basic farming infrastructure on which all subsequent development in Exmoor was built (Orwin and Sellick 1970: 98).

IMPROVEMENT AND THE RISE AND FALL OF ROBERT SMITH

Exmoor could not be made profitable simply by constructing new farmsteads and hiring willing tenants. Farming itself needed to become more productive to generate the funds for further improvement. It was also during the 1840s and 1850s that discussion about the 'hidden fertility' of Exmoor dominated agricultural journals and public debates. Most notably, in 1843, Phillip Pusey's article in the *Journal of the Royal Agricultural Society* argued that the 'modern methods' and 'scientific principals' used for the reclamation of the Lincolnshire heathlands should be extended to Exmoor (Pusey 1843). The article was republished multiple times in various local and national newspapers, where it may have caught Frederic Knight's attention (*Western Times*, 4 May 1850; *Salisbury and Winchester Journal*, 25 October 1851). He decided that the 'reclamation' of Exmoor now required an 'improved' and 'knowledgeable' tenantry to apply cutting-edge 'scientific' agriculture. Consequently, in 1848, John Mogridge was replaced as steward by Robert Smith of Lincolnshire. A darling of the agricultural commentariat, Smith's career is detailed by Orwin and Sellick. In summary, Smith belonged to an established Lincolnshire farming family, and although only in his late thirties, he had already established himself as a breeder of Shorthorn cattle and Leicester sheep, as well as as an agricultural essayist. A founder of the Rutland Agricultural Society, he also served on the councils of both the Royal Agricultural Society and the Bath and West of England Society, where he was a dogged champion of Lincolnshire farming methods (Orwin and Sellick 1970: 73–97). Frederic Knight decided that Robert Smith would be the perfect choice to bring 'modern farming' to Exmoor, even though he lacked any practical experience as a steward and had previously managed only a single farm. Nevertheless, Frederic Knight lavished praise upon his new steward, as 'one of the best, cleverest and most enlightened farmers in England'. Frederic boasted to his father:

> You would be much pleased with the way in which Robert Smith is attacking the Emmett's. Draining, breaking and covering lime in a way the Forest has not seen for many years. He will have 100 acres of corn next year! (SHC A/EJM/1/1/6 Frederic Knight to John Knight, 13 March 1848; Frederic Knight to John Knight, 15 September 1848)

In local newspapers, commentators praised Knight for abandoning his father's methods, and devoted space to the 'innovations' that Smith had brought to the 'backward' moorland (*Western Times*, 6 November 1841, 28 October 1848; *Salisbury and Winchester Journal*, 25 October 1851). As William Hannam, tenant of Cornham Farm, acknowledged in his memoirs by the mid-1840s, there was 'so much conversation in the neighbourhood respecting Exmoor Farms … I had a great inclination to see it' (Orwin and Sellick 1970: 243). Within a few years of inheriting the estate, Frederic Knight had thus managed to reignite belief in Exmoor's hidden potential.

The advent of Robert Smith revived discourses of internal colonialism, and so both he and Frederic Knight sought to populate the new farms with 'industrious' and 'civilized' tenants. Influenced by Pusey's views about the 'superior quality' of heathland farming, Knight and Smith focused their search within recently enclosed areas of Lincolnshire,

Leicestershire and South Yorkshire, and prospective tenants were referred to repeatedly in their correspondence as 'Midlands' farmers (see Williams 1970). This fascination with 'foreign expertise' was predicated on the belief that local people were incapable of innovation, and a prejudice against those who had traditionally grazed animals on the Royal Forest (Sidney 1878: 79). Furthermore, these derogatory claims were reinforced by early experiences. When the farms were first let, John Mogridge and Frederic Knight had attempted to recruit dairy farmers from Dorset because of their experience working with poor soils. This included William Hannam at Cornham, Henry Hibberd at Emmett's Grange, Henry Matthews at Honeymead, Edwin Godwin at Simonsbath Barton and the Dulley brothers at Duredon and Wintershead. However, it was soon apparent that these men were unwilling to invest in long-term improvements, because they were used to operating on the tight margins of dairy farming. Frederic Knight's disdain for West Country farmers was compounded by negative experiences such as Hibberd suing him for breach of covenant and the Dulleys absconding due to rent arrears (French and Baker 2023; Orwin and Sellick 1970: 258). In 1848, Frederic told his father that:

> I have no doubt of the ultimate success of the Forest if we get the best of the Lincoln Heath men on and hold the property for 20 years. They are cultivators. The Dorsetshire dairymen are not. Their secret is to make some profit off poor grasses without spending any money. (SHC A/EJM/1/1/6 Frederic Knight to John Knight, 15 September 1848)

Such passages illustrate the connections drawn between cultivation and civilisation and the perception of locals as exploiters or despoilers. They echo descriptions of Ireland and America, where 'uncivilized and rebellious locals' were held responsible for rendering fertile land inhospitable and unprofitable (Pluymers 2011; Dezateux Robson 2024). These prejudices were shared by successive land agents on Exmoor, and influenced their hiring practices, day-to-day operations and perceptions of 'reclamation'. Robert Smith would add his own romantic spin by claiming he needed a tenantry who could achieve 'permanent improvement' through 'forced spirits and bodily strength' (SHC A/EJM/1/3/7 Robert Smith to Frederic Knight, 21 February 1852). He argued that efforts to 'redeem the property' necessitated a continuous investment of 'time, energy and capital', by a tenantry who was knowledgeable enough in the 'agricultural sciences' to 'go on making the permanent and other improvements at the rate I have hitherto done' (SHC A/EJM/1/3/8 Robert Smith to Frederic Knight, 2 February 1853). In fact, during this period, many of these 'ideal' tenants were also potential emigres. In May 1846, Frederic Knight was encouraged to offer Thomas Walker, of Market Weighton, Yorkshire, a favourable tenancy agreement 'as soon as possible as he has contemplated going to America if he does not come here' (SHC A/EJM/1/1/7 John Mogridge to Frederic Knight, 30 May 1846). In contrast, local farmers' resistance to new methods was often ridiculed:

> Bone and Lime will astonish the natives of Exmoor ... I purchased 8 tons of oil cake for myself and people about me thought me rather mad, but when he talks of buying 100 ton a year they would have had him confined at once in a lunatic asylum. (SHC A/EJM/1/3/18 Frederic Smyth to Frederic Knight, 3 January 1868)

By 1853, an anonymous letter to the *North Devon Journal* reported that there was 'not a Devon or Somerset man amongst us' and that everyone currently on the estate had been 'allured from a distance, at first with the hope of gain' (*NDJ*, 10 March 1853).

Yet, analysis of the tenants who were outsiders suggests that, in practice, Smith and Knight were forced to lower their standards (French and Baker 2023). This was driven by the financial pressures on Frederic Knight. When John Knight died in 1850, he gave the Exmoor estate to Frederic but required him to pay legacies to his siblings based on its overall value. This created an immediate and long-lasting battle in Chancery, in which his brothers and sisters alleged that the estate was worth far more than its annual income would suggest. This deprived Frederic of full control of the estate until 1862 and made him desperate for a source of reliable income (Orwin and Sellick 1970: 101; SHC A/EJM/1/1/3 Frederic Knight to Lady Headley, n.d. 1852). The urgent need for rents drove Smith to scour the Midlands and South Yorkshire for anyone willing to take an Exmoor farm. Newspapers such as the *Stamford Mercury* featured advertisements offering 'liberal leases, tenant-right on unexhausted improvements, and a low scale of rents' (*Stamford Mercury*, 3 Feb. 1854). Additionally, Smith raided his personal and familial contacts. Between 1847 and 1857, Smith recruited 11 farmers from Lincolnshire, Leicestershire, Yorkshire, Derbyshire and Warwickshire, all of whom took on substantial new farms on the estate. They included his brother-in-law, Robert Searson, from

Deeping St. James; Lincolnshire, who took on Horsen Farm; William Minnett, from Barkston near Grantham on the Lincolnshire heathlands, who tenanted Driver Farm; and John Bullas from Cantley, near Doncaster in Yorkshire, who farmed Duredon (TNA HO 107/617/4 1841 Census, Robert Searson; TNA RG09/2482/15 1861 Census, William Minnett; TNA HO 107/1330/111841 Census, John Bullas).

However, many were not the brilliant colonists Smith and Knight had envisaged. For example, John Knight's former seat at Simonsbath House Farm was let to Charles Le Blanc, a lawyer from Epsom who had no previous experience in farming. He had been recruited on the word of a single referee, whose lukewarm reference described him as being 'equal to the farm, at least so far as he knows and the only drawback is that he is separated from his wife' (SHC A/EJM/1/3/6 Robert Smith to Frederic Knight, 22 May 1851). Similarly, George Allen Harrold, who took Warren Farm, impressed Smith with the capital he was willing to invest, but his previous profession was as a wholesale gentleman's outfitter in Leicester. Due to their inexperience, both Le Blanc and Harrold were reliant upon bailiffs, also from the Midlands, to run their farms, neither of whom proved successful (Orwin and Sellick 1970: 264; SHC A/EJM/1/3/6 Charles Le Blanc to Frederic Knight, 3 September 1851). In contrast, Charles Popple, from Sculcoates near Hull, attempted to farm Simonsbath Barton alone. Prior to Exmoor, he had been a partner in an oilcake business and manager of a cotton factory, but failed in both (Bellamy 1962; French and Baker 2023). Consequently, these 'Midlands' tenants were a motley collection, ranging from wealthy farmers and businessmen who could take a farm as a speculative venture, to desperate men hoping that Exmoor could change their fortunes.

Despite the hiring of outside cultivators and the adoption of Robert Smith's 'scientific' techniques, the pace of 'reclamation' slowed between 1848 and 1862. As noted previously, under Frederic Knight, there were only 52 acts of large-scale drainage and irrigation, in contrast to the 151 individual entries recorded between 1818 and 1843. Although this can be explained partially by the switch to tenant farming, which removed drainage and irrigation from the estate accounts, archaeological surveys and analysis of the estate's correspondence confirm that under Robert Smith, efforts were limited to drainage maintenance or the 'improvement' of individual fields (Riley 2019; Baker et al. 2024). Between 1848 and 1862, large-scale reclamation was stymied by the inability of the estate to invest, the tenants' lack of capital, and Smith's preference for fashionable but undertested and expensive 'scientific' grassland improvement, rather than mundane but vital agricultural necessities such as drainage or fencing. Critically, despite the shift towards 'independent' tenant farmers, Smith still attempted to dictate reclamation policy. Inspired by reports of 'high farming' or reclamation systems adopted in Yorkshire, Lincolnshire, Leicestershire and Derbyshire, Smith tried to apply a 'modification of the [reclamation] system of all those districts' to the farms on Exmoor (SHC A/EJM/1/1/6 Robert Smith to William Fowler, 3 November 1849; *Illustrated London News*, 19 October 1853). His 'plan of reclamation' was to first drain and break up the land, spreading at least '2½ to 3 tons of lime per acre' followed by a 'crop of turnips sown on the flat' to be 'eaten off with sheep' with the land finally 'pastured for three years' and then either kept as pasture or ploughed for arable (Sidney 1878; Smith 1856). Unsurprisingly, this method imitated the schemes featured in articles written by Pusey and other influential members of the Royal Agricultural Society (Pusey 1841; Johnson 1841; Watson 1845).

Although drainage and irrigation remained integral to the reclamation process, Smith's methods were a decisive shift away from John Knight's plan. This was praised by Smith's contemporaries as a return to 'practical knowledge' that could 'sustain the productiveness of the land' (Darby 1873). Smith's 'high farming' approach required closer attention to soil preparation through repeated and intensive liming and extensive cultivation of turnips as winter fodder to be eaten 'in field' by sheep stocks (Orwin and Sellick 1970: 104–9). Moreover, Smith abandoned John Knight's (landlord-driven) landscape-scale improvements in favour of (tenant-led) preparation of specific fields around the new farmsteads. Although Smith's plans were much more limited geographically than John Knight's, they remained labour intensive, financially prohibitive and environmentally disruptive. Smith's own accounts show that it took four years of hard labour to 'improve' Cottage Field, a single field of 16 acres (6.5 ha), to accommodate his agricultural system. This included repeatedly digging and maintaining open-cut drainage, eliminating headsprings, two courses of subsoiling, and multiple courses of lime each season. Excluding the lime, Smith estimated that it had cost him £47 19s. Whilst this was being achieved, 16 other fields were being similarly transformed on Smith's holdings at Emmett's Grange, Long Holcombe and Western Emmett's (SHC A/EJM/1/3/5 Expenditure by Tenant on Emmett's Farm 1849–1853). Extrapolating from Smith's 1856 essay on improving moorland, and including the 'constant courses of lime', it would cost £4

5s per acre to improve 'rough moorland' (Orwin and Sellick 1970: 87; Smith 1856: 379–83). At Emmett's Grange, Smith spent £927 1s 9d on reclamation projects with very little return in either capital or crops (SHC A/EJM/1/3/5 Statement of Expenditure ... 1849–1853). As William Hannam, a tenant at Cornham, recalled:

> Mr Smith began to Attempt things that was Quite unreasonable for the Climate. He attempted to Grow Wheat several seasons I hird him say one Year he had 20 Acres ... I was at his House repeatedley and I never saw a loaf of Bread made with it neither have I in the 12 Years I have bin on the Moor seen a Loaf of Bread fit for aney one to eat ... (Orwin and Sellick 1970: 261)

Although personal animosity may have biased these observations, private correspondence between Smith and Knight indicates that Smith's ambitious reclamation schemes were financially unsustainable. In February 1853, Smith revealed that he had run out of capital and that 'we can make no return during the winter season and the limited return we have in the summer is taken up by labour'. This left him no choice: 'My course *must* be to stay my hand, as it is quite impossible for me to go on making the permanent and other improvements at the rate I have hitherto done' (SHC A/EJM/1/3/8 Robert Smith to Frederic Knight, 2 February 1853). By 1856, Smith asked Knight for personal loans to keep him solvent until the next livestock fair (SHC A/EJM/1/3/10 Robert Smith to Frederic Knight, 28 January 1856; SHC A/EJM/1/3/11 William Fowler to Frederic Knight, 2 February 1856). Such financial difficulties reveal the treacherous conditions for farmers on Exmoor, especially as Smith was supposed to be the most capable and had his independent wage as steward to fall back on.

Smith reconciled his desire to implement a strict new farming system across the estate with Frederic Knight's hands-off approach, by using leases to lock the tenantry into adopting his improvement schemes. Under Smith's plan for reclamation, the financial burden of enacting 'permanent improvements' was passed to the tenantry who were promised compensation in the form of 'liberal leases' or rent abatements if they managed to meet the standards set on Smith's 'show-farm' at Emmett's Grange. Rent rebates were offered 'if the tenant drains the land at his own expense', 'for lime used on the land', 'for bones used on the land', 'for subsoiling peat lands', 'for making and planting new fences', 'for the making of water-meadows', 'for buildings erected on the land' (SHC A/BAZ/1/4 Tenant Contract Detailing Permanent Improvements; SHC A/EJM/1/3/7

Robert Smith to Frederic Knight, 21 February 1852). Moreover, individual tenants were expected to follow Robert Smith's instructions for any 'necessary work' that he believed was necessary on their farm. For example, Charles Le Blanc at Simonsbath House was required to complete the following tasks to qualify for repayments:

> Roads to be put in tenantable repair and kept so by the tenant. Fences, to be estimated and repaired (as requested) by tenant and repaid at succeeding rent day. Buildings as above (for fences), cart shed to be roofed, general buildings adjusted for the rest of the farm and the present mill house to be enlarged for a barn at a future period but done by tenant. (SHC A/ EJM/1/3/6 Robert Smith to Frederic Knight, 20 May 1851)

In addition, Knight and Smith assumed that any prospective tenant on Exmoor must be willing to lose money for at least two years, whilst also having the funds to invest in fencing and intensive liming. Even then, Knight acknowledged that it would take at least '20 years' for permanent improvement to take hold (SHC A/EJM/1/1/6 Frederic Knight to John Knight, 15 September 1848). Tenants were often faced with impossible targets to qualify for a repayment. For example, Gerard Spooner's lease of Wintershead Farm required him to improve a quarter of the land he rented (300 acres/121 ha). Smith's own calculations in his agricultural articles on 'improving moorland', imply that Spooner needed to spend £1275 in his first four years (Orwin and Sellick 1970: 87). Moreover, deviations from these covenants were quickly suppressed. As William Hannam noted, when he attempted to continue dairying 'I was pirswaded by Mr Smith and maney others to keep some Sheep and less Dairey' (Orwin and Sellick 1970: 266). In response, Smith wrote that forcing this switch would lead to 'some permanent improvements being made' and, eventually, the tenants would 'speak and act accordingly' as 'spirited and satisfied men' (SHC A/EJM/1/3/7 Robert Smith to Frederic Knight, 11 February 1852). It appears, therefore, that Smith's improvement plans also sought to inculcate a new sense of industry amongst the tenantry (Image 2).

With the tenantry now tasked with the 'everyday' duties of liming, irrigation and drainage through their 'liberal covenants', Robert Smith could focus on larger schemes, particularly the 'catch-water meadows' highlighted in Pusey's 1849 report for the Royal Agricultural Society (Pusey 1849). As noted previously, these hillside meadows had been used on Exmoor and the surrounding regions for centuries. However, this article described catch meadows as a 'triumph of agricultural art' and placed

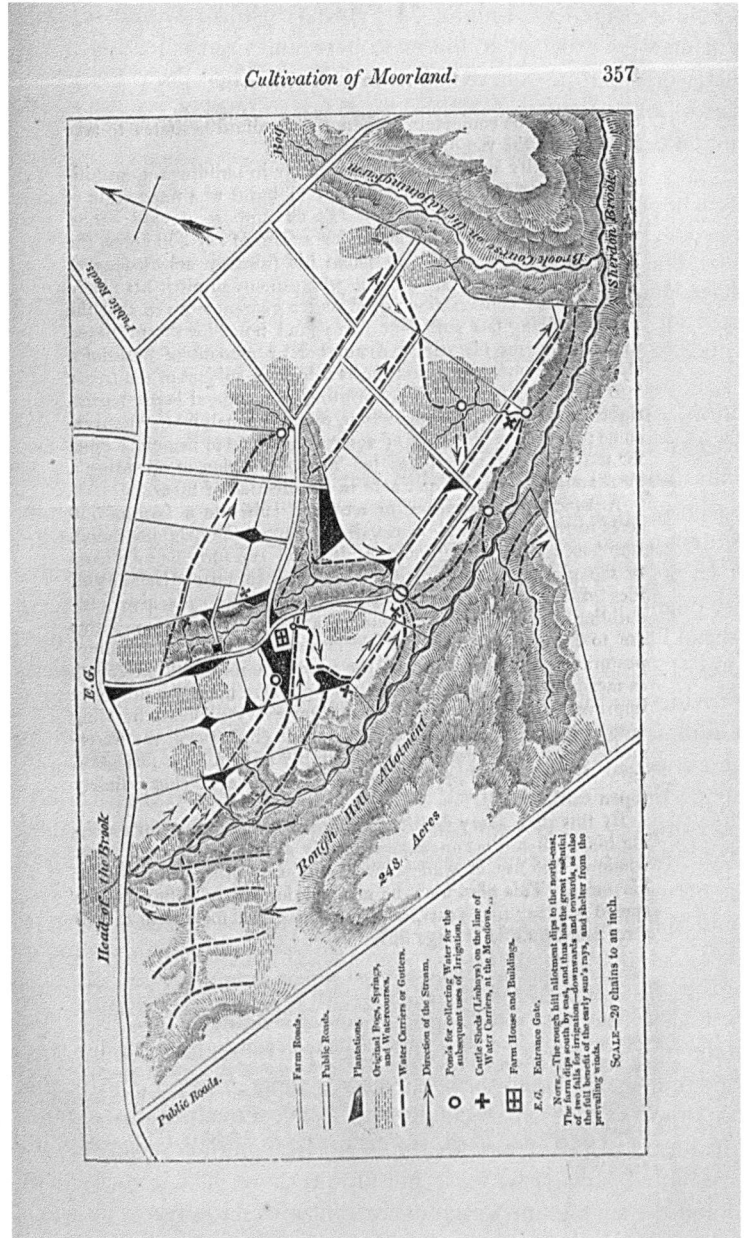

Image 2 Robert Smith, 'Bringing Moorland into Cultivation', *Journal of the Royal Agricultural Society of England*, 17 (1856), p. 357. (Source: https://www.biodiversitylibrary.org/item/37121 (accessed 6 August 2024))

them at the heart of Smith's 'scientific' improvement of Exmoor. In a private letter, Smith concluded that 'nature's chief dictate is the water-meadow—few estates have such natural facilities for their formation' (SHC A/EJM/1/1/6 Robert Smith to William Fowler, 3 November 1848), but its widespread use by locals was minimised and denigrated by nineteenth-century agriculturalists. They claimed that the water-meadows created by 'rustic forefathers' had been undermined by numerous 'intricate faults' that had remained until 'new designs suggested themselves' to Robert Smith (Pusey 1849; Smith 1856). As such, the construction of an 'improved' water-meadow beside each new farmstead on Exmoor became a public advertisement for the latest in agricultural 'improvement'. In national newspapers, new farms were advertised specifically for their 'extensive irrigation by means of catch-meadows', which promised occupiers 'unexhausted improvements' to the 'native grasses' (*Bell's Weekly Messenger*, 3 September 1849). Critically, these claims were not purely cynical marketing, and William Hannam argued that the estate frequently prioritised the construction of water-meadows to its own detriment:

> I think Mr Knight in time will see that Mr Smith has spent scores of Pounds usesley in Cutting Gutters to take water on that is a Newsance to the Land instead of a Benifitt—I do not think that the Bog water taken of the Hill that have never bin Broken or Limed and turned on the Land that has been Limed can be of aney Benifitt … I believe Mr Smith made a great mistake in neglecting the Fences to Drayn the Bogs and spending a deal of Money in Cutting Gutters for Catch Meadows. (Orwin and Sellick 1970: 260)

Water-meadows and irrigation schemes across the moorland propagandised a narrative of economic, social and environmental change, and influential commentators turned them into hallmarks of modern and industrious farming. Robert Smith's reputation (and career prospects) depended on sustaining such a narrative, so he prioritised such schemes over more mundane but more important tasks, such as fencing and repairing drains.

TENANTS AND THE BURDENS OF IMPROVEMENT

Smith's desire to 'conquer the rugged moor' at any cost combined with overly optimistic estimations of Exmoor's potential and the neglect of everyday infrastructure to create a volatile situation for the largely inexperienced and unsupported new tenantry (SHC A/EJM/1/3/7 Robert

Smith to Frederic Knight, 19 March 1852). The frantic pace of farm building between 1844 and 1852 meant that many tenants arrived to find their holdings incomplete and unsuitable for habitation and agriculture. Most notably, in 1847, Henry Hibberd arrived at Emmett's Grange Farm to discover that the farmhouse, labourers' cottages, granary and cattle sheds were all unfinished. With their new home lacking floors, stairs, windows and plastered walls, Hibberd and his family were forced to lodge in the kitchen and dining room of Simonsbath House. During this time, half of Hibberd's cattle herd died of exposure due to a lack of shelter, leaving him financially ruined. Unsurprisingly, Hibberd quit Exmoor and sued Frederic Knight for a breach of covenant. In his defence, Knight argued that Hibberd had been an incompetent farmer who had failed to use lime or invest in his farm (French and Baker 2023):

> I had before cautioned him against taking it without sufficient capital: I told him he would be doing me great injury if he did, and that he could not expect to pay his rent out of the farm for the first two years … In my judgement it would have required a great deal of capital property to cultivate that farm—£3000 would at the least be required … he said he had capital enough to keep a dairy farm where the land was prepared for it, but not enough to go on with the farm on Exmoor. (*NDJ*, 19 August 1847)

Although Knight won the case, his claim that £3000 and two years without income was required reveals the huge financial demands placed on new tenants. This was exacerbated by the estate's willingness to take on new tenants with far less capital. In the previous year, John Hedditch had been allowed to rent Driver Farm (400 acres/162 ha) for £200 per annum despite Mogridge reporting that 'from what I can find he has about £700 which I think with his industry he will be able to do well' (SHC A/EJM/1/1/2 John Mogridge to Frederic Knight, 22 September 1846).

Throughout the next decade, many tenants failed because they lost vital stock and crops from inadequate shelter, fencing, drainage and infrastructure. William Hannam noted that inadequate fencing damaged Henry Matthews' plans to keep both cattle and sheep at Honeymead, because 'the fences not being up in a proper manner … the sheep would consume the best pasture from the Cows and he found he could make butt little from them' (Orwin and Sellick 1970: 255). Indeed, despite it being one of centrepieces of Smith's article on 'moorland cultivation', between 1848 and 1862, tenants were constantly complaining about inadequate fencing (Smith 1856). In 1851, Charles Le Blanc would write to Frederic Knight to report.

> I fear, I have no sufficient fence to keep out Mr Harrold's sheep, but that these are seen during the winter months to descend upon the 40 acres of land, which I have of late at great expense broken up, and to devour all the food upon it. (SHC A/EJM/1/3/6 Charles Le Blanc to Frederic Knight, 5 September 1851)

George Allen Harrold threatened to quit Exmoor 'because he had already lost £1000 ... and that we would not meet him in the Boundary Fences' (SHC A/EJM/1/3/8 Robert Smith to Frederic Knight, 4 January 1853). Even the most promising and experienced farmers found their plans ruined by these oversights. For example, Gerard Spooner had previously run a successful farm in Scotland, and his arrival in 1852 drew the attention of local newspapers when he landed at Ilfracombe with 1200 young ewes (SHC A/EJM/1/3/7 Robert Smith to Frederic Knight, 24 March 1852; *Western Times,* 17 July 1852). However, during the winter of 1853, a lack of barns and linhays cost Spooner most of his flock (SHC A/EJM/1/3/8 Robert Smith to Frederic Knight, 9 February 1853). This ruined his plans, and by 1856, he wanted to leave Exmoor, having made only the most minor 'improvements' to his land (SHC A/EJM/1/3/12 Robert Smith to William Fowler, 19 September 1856). By this time, even Smith was forced to acknowledge that his efforts to incentivise tenants to conduct expensive 'permanent improvements' through rent rebates were failing. In August 1856, he reported to Knight that the 'disbursement accounts' to the tenants are 'much lighter than formerly' and the pace of work had slowed considerably across the estate (SHC A/EJM/1/3/12 Robert Smith to Frederic Knight, 27 August 1856). Unsurprisingly, whatever their previous experience or capital, few of the new tenants could afford to begin long-term reclamation projects when they were constantly on the brink of financial disaster.

The perception that Exmoor was a secretly productive *tabula rasa* also ensured that tenants were given far more land than they could cultivate, and rents were set according to (optimistic) future projections of what land *would* be worth rather than what it was. The assumption was that although tenants would lose money initially, they would recoup it over the course of their lease, but in practice, it ensured that many were saddled with unsustainable debts. For example, in 1851, Charles Le Blanc blamed his troubles on being given 'superfluous land of 240 acres' that was 'at too high a rent, too unprotected and too little divided by fences' (SHC A/ EJM/1/3/6 Charles Le Blanc to Frederic Knight, 3 September 1851). Although some farmers, such as Meadows 'sold a verey good Propertey in Leastershire' to invest in his farm at Larkbarrow, others were in much more precarious circumstances. George Groves, of Pinkery Farm, was described as an 'Invaleed' who was deeply indebted even before he arrived (Orwin and Sellick 1970: 264). Consequently, among the first generation of tenants only Henry Matthews at Honeymead and Robert Smith at Emmett's Grange managed to last the '20 years' that Frederic Knight estimated it would take to achieve 'permanent improvement' (SHC A/ EJM/1/1/6 Frederic Knight to John Knight, 15 September 1848). The next closest, William Hannam of Cornham, only managed to last 12 years due to the subsidies and support from Robert Smith, who wished to avoid an embarrassing public failure. As we have detailed elsewhere, of the 18 tenants on Exmoor farms between 1842 and 1868 from Dorset, Wiltshire and the Midlands, only six survived beyond the first six-year interval of the standard lease. Six became insolvent because of their time on Exmoor (James Coombs at Crooked Post, James Meadows at Larkbarrow, Charles Popple at Simonsbath Barton, John Hedditch at Driver and William Wood at Warren Farm), and George Groves committed suicide at his farm at Goat Hill (Orwin and Sellick 1970: 264; French and Baker 2023). Two others (the Dulley brothers) absconded with some of their stock, and their fate is unknown (Orwin and Sellick 1970: 258). Another six Exmoor farmers went on to farm elsewhere, some returning to their home county and taking on (or returning to) farms of 100–300 acres (40–121 ha), including John Hedditch, whose possessions on Exmoor were sold to satisfy his creditors, while Gerard Spooner went much further afield, emigrating to New Zealand in 1860 (SHC A/EJM/1/3/7 Robert Smith to Frederic Knight, 20 February 1852; 'Biography of Gerard Spooner'). John Bullas, who farmed at Duredon for seven years and was described as a 'hard working, industrious man and hauling lime on his farm well', returned to Yorkshire to become a butcher (SHC A/BAZ/1/8 William Howchin to Frederic Knight, 16 May 1852; TNA RG 10/4720/39 1871 Census, John Bullas). As these examples indicate, catastrophic failure and financial ruin were commonplace and could strike even the most skilled tenant.

The previous experience of this first generation of tenant farmers on Exmoor in soil improvement or farming mattered little when farm buildings were unfinished, there was insufficient land for growing fodder or roots and basic infrastructure, such as drains and fences, was inadequate. These issues amplified other problems, such as the harsh winters and the isolation of Exmoor and made it more difficult for tenants to draw on traditional forms of family support (French and Baker 2023). However, Robert Smith and Frederic Knight were slow to recognise the systemic or institutional causes for the repeated misfortunes and failures of the tenantry. Instead, Smith attributed these to their personal failings, particularly the lack of industry and intellect. When Charles Le Blanc complained about the state of his farm in 1858, Smith argued that his skills were 'inadequate' and his failure to produce any good crops was due to his lime being 'improperly applied' (SHC A/EJM/1/3/14 Robert Smith to Frederic Knight, 10 May 1858). Similarly, Smith repeatedly accused William Hannam of being incompetent and lazy, claiming that his desire to continue dairying on Exmoor would be a 'complete loss' and would cause him to 'lose interest' in his farm and making improvements (SHC A/EJM/1/3/6 Robert Smith to Frederic Knight, 15 May 1851, 1 June 1851, 18 September 1851). As with Frederic Knight's critiques of Hibberd, blaming the moral failings of the tenants enabled Smith to protect his own reputation. Smith had presented the tenants of Exmoor as modern, industrious and scientific farmers in his writings and dealings with the agricultural commentariat, and any notable failures jeopardised this image. However, many of the suffering tenants laid the blame at Smith's door. William Hannam concluded:

> I think he, Mr Smith, expected to gett a lott of Gentleman Farmers Resident as Farmers to join with him I sopose with his Hounds and Keep him Companey regardless at whose expence it may be or whom he ruined. (Orwin and Sellick 1970: 266)

During this period, Frederic Knight was largely absent from Exmoor, and these repeated agrarian misfortunes and failures made him ever more anxious to find other ways of making the estate profitable, rather as John Knight had pinned his hopes on the promised family inheritance. By 1856, Robert Smith had also shifted his attention away from agriculture, in the hope that 'reclamation' could be supported by the estate's supposed mineral wealth (Bray 2010; Orwin and Sellick 1970: 170–221). Primed by

Smith, in the mid-1850s, local and national newspapers reported that a fortune in iron ore was awaiting any industrious prospector, rather as contemporaries also believed they could unlock the 'hidden fertility' of the moorland (*Devizes and Wiltshire Gazette*, 26 June 1856). Smith invested quickly in this new venture, building himself a mineral 'laboratory' at Emmett's Grange and inviting multiple mining companies, most notably the Dowlais Mining Company of South Wales, to begin digging exploratory shafts across the moorland (SHC A/EJM/1/3/12 Robert Smith to Frederic Knight, 26 May 1856, 29 May 1856, 22 August 1856). However, the search for a profitable vein proved to be illusory, and by August 1857, the Dowlais Company had realised that none of the iron veins detected were rich enough to justify the expense of industrial-scale mining (SHC A/EJM/1/3/12 Robert Smith to Frederic Knight, 27 August 1856; Orwin and Sellick 1970: 200–4). This failure ended Robert Smith's hopes that his style of farming could be supported on Exmoor by an outside source of income (SHC A/BAZ/1/4 Draft Letter from Frederic Knight to the *Pall Mall Gazette*, c. 1880 [1883]).

This was also the final blow to the relationship between Frederic Knight and Robert Smith. Without investment from the Dowlais Company, the Exmoor Railway extension from Minehead was also cancelled, along with the cheap transportation of large quantities of lime that Frederic Knight had been campaigning for since he inherited the estate (SHC DD/BR/BN/31 Exmoor and Porlock Railways 1826–1860; *Daily News*, 11 November 1859). In fact, the estate correspondence reveals that their relationship had been fractious and combative since the mid-1850s. In 1856, Smith complained bitterly that he was not 'allowed to pay my Lady Day Rent at the same time as the other tenants and receive my half-year's salary when due'. It seems that Frederic Knight did not take these requests seriously, simply annotating the letter: 'Smith: On your money or your life!' (SHC A/EJM/1/3/10 Robert Smith to Frederic Knight, 28 January 1856). Equally, Knight would often simply fail to reply to Smith, meaning that vital requests for wages or financial support went unanswered. At the same time, Smith was expected to maintain Emmett's as a 'show farm', which led to several complaints:

> I feel much averse to enter upon comparisons, otherwise I could dwell at some length upon the state of other tenants farms, fences, arrears of rent, amount of lime, drawn and etc in comparison with my own hitherto costly

'show farm' for the good of the property … If Mr Knight is displeased with me, I should prefer his saying so, that I might render him full explanations rather than hurt any feelings at a moment when I require every help and support he can give, both as regards the farm and agency. (SHC A/ EJM/1/3/10 Robert Smith to William Fowler, 17 April 1856)

By 1859, correspondence between Robert Smith and Frederic Knight had almost completely evaporated. Indeed, by this time, Smith was essentially running the estate by himself, arguing in one letter that 'unless you do give me an answer to these requests, I shall be fully justified in making my own selection and go on with my farming' (SHC A/EJM/1/3/15 Robert Smith to Frederic Knight, 9 March 1859). By early 1861, the relationship ended, and Smith was dismissed as steward at Lady Day (25 March) that year. This produced a public spat between Smith and Knight, through a series of letters to the local newspapers. In the first, an 'anonymous' writer claimed that 'the severance of Mr Smith's connexion with the property has cast a gloom over the tenantry'. This drew an immediate retort from Frederic Knight, who stated that Smith did not resign, but 'I felt it necessary to dismiss him from the agency' (*NDJ*, 21 March 1861, 28 March 1861, 4 April 1861). Although Smith would continue at Emmett's Grange for seven more years, this marked the end of his attempts to reclaim the moorland (Orwin and Sellick 1970: 115–20).

THE RETURN OF 'IN-COUNTY' FARMERS

As the first generation of Dorset and Midlands tenants departed after 1856–1857, they were replaced by farmers from North Devon and north Somerset, who always predominated thereafter. This change was barely discussed between Smith and Knight, or in contemporary publications, but the cultivation of Exmoor only really stabilised and achieved a modest level of profitability with the advent of farmers who could draw on the personal and financial resources of local familial networks and farms (Orwin and Sellick 1970: 101–2). Ironically, Robert Smith himself had hinted at this in his 1856 publication, 'Bringing Moorland into Cultivation' (Smith 1856). While the article focused on his own efforts at Emmett's Grange, particularly the construction of outbuildings and catch meadows, Smith remarked, in passing, that:

A tenant who proposes to rent and cultivate a farm of 300 acres of rough hill land is usually a man of the neighbourhood, who has a heart for 'roughing it' and can turn his own hand to the plough when wanted. (Smith 1856: 361)

While most tenants were not locals in 1856, by the end of the decade, Smith was letting most of the farms and other allotments to those who were. He was even willing to split up such holdings to make them more attractive and affordable to locals, an anathema when the estate sought capital from prosperous Midlanders. Local tenants could use newly enclosed moorland allotments as summer grazing for farms adjacent to the moor, despite this running counter to the estate's earlier hopes for 'permanent' reclamation. Sub-divided estate farms required less capital outlay because they contained smaller areas to fence and lime. In 1857, Smith informed Knight that he had broken up Charles Le Blanc's large but dispersed holding in Simonsbath. 'The remaining parts of the farm I have estimated in fields for the cottages and others, and the allotments would be let to in-county farmers' (SHC A/EJM/1/3/13 Robert Smith to Frederic Knight, 6 August 1857). Smith's new-found tolerance of 'in-county' farmers resulted from his failure to attract properly capitalised outsiders, prepared to invest in Exmoor through his 'improving leases'. It may also have reflected his growing frustration with Exmoor and Frederic Knight (SHC A/EJM/1/3/10 Robert Smith to William Fowler, 17 April 1856). Whatever Smith or Knight thought about them, local tenants seemed better able to pay their rents than outsiders, even if it meant abandoning earlier dreams of 'high farming'. For example, in negotiating with Edwin Maunder, a wool merchant turned farmer from Headley Village, North Molton, Smith had to accept Maunder's demand for rough grazing as summer pasture for sheep he kept elsewhere, without the expense of renting a farm that he had to improve.

Mr Maunder even declines the 300 acres at 7/6 single handed, on account of the continued outlay that must annually be gone into, for the improvement of the fields. (SHC A/EJM/1/3/8 Robert Smith to Frederic Knight, 17 September 1858)

In this period, several farms were sub-divided, including Crooked Post, Honeymead, Simonsbath House Farm, Goat Hill, and Picked Stones (SHC A/EJM/6/2 Knight Estate Receivers' Accounts 1852–1862). Larkbarrow, Tom's Hill and Duredon were resumed by the estate and turned over to shepherds for the in-hand sheep ranching that began under the stewardship of Smith's replacement, Frederic Smyth, in the mid-1860s (DHC 1262M/0/E/20/152 Fortescue of Castle Hill Estate Exmoor Estate Rentals 1864–1875; 1262M/0/E/20/153 Exmoor Estate Rentals 1875–1886).

By this time, other observers noticed the positive effects of agrarian change in the area and praised their civilising influences. In the late 1850s, Exmoor-raised cattle began to win prizes at local agricultural shows, and in 1858, the famous hunting-parson Rev. John (Jack) Russell observed to the Bishop's Tawton Agricultural Society that:

> It had been said that North Devon was 100 years behind other parts the country in agricultural improvement; but he had lately heard Mr. Knight, of Exmoor, say that he had let a farm for which he had several tenders of £300 a year, and he believed that 20 years ago the district could not have produced a man to offer a rent £300 a year. This was to him (Mr. R.) a proof that North Devon farmers had been improving—that they were as intelligent, enterprising, and respectable as any of their class, come from what part of England they might. (*NDJ*, 14 January 1858, 23 September 1858)

Table 1 details the county of origin of tenants taking up leases on the estate in the period covered by the estate's annual accounts (1852–1886). 107 of the 134 tenants (80 per cent) originated from the two counties bordering Exmoor, and virtually all tenants were locals after the mid-1860s (French and Baker 2023). This marked a profound shift from the pattern in the late 1840s. Cross-referencing to local censuses demonstrates that just over 70 per cent of tenants were either farmers or agricultural labourers (often the sons of farmers working on their father's farms, or those in the neighbourhood).

The public firing of Smith, alongside the dramatic failures of some tenants, led to growing debate about the value of Exmoor and 'home colonies'. Belief in the inevitable success of a 'home colony' on Exmoor quickly evaporated once 'improvement' of the moorland stalled in the 1850s. By the early 1860s, even committed 'improvers' and agriculturalists were questioning the wisdom of these projects. In 1857, a public debate was held in response to a paper given by Robert Smith regarding 'waste lands and home colonies' where it was concluded that 'there is something very pretty in the idea of home colonies, but there is nothing practical'. Despite all his work, it was the sheer expense of Robert Smith's work on Exmoor that undermined belief in the value of 'home colonies':

Table 1 Number of tenants arriving on Exmoor from various English counties in 5-year periods between 1852 and 1889

County of Origin	1850–1854	1855–1859	1860–1864	1865–1869	1870–1874	1875–1879	1880–1884	1885–1889	Total N
Derbyshire	1								1
Devon	4	6	14	12	8	8	11	17	80
Dorset	2								2
Leicestershire	1	1							2
Lincolnshire		2	1						3
Middlesex				1				1	2
Northants				1					1
Somerset	1	2	4	3	5	4	2	6	27
Surrey			2						2
Sussex			1						1
Warwickshire		1							1
Yorkshire	1		1	1					3
Unknown		2	1	3	1			2	9
Total N	10	14	24	21	14	12	13	26	134

Those who call for home colonies, in effect, ask the government to spend a hundred million in introducing the agriculture of the dark ages, and creating a colony of paupers, planted on soil where they would sow guineas and reap halfpence. (*Oxford Chronicle and Reading Gazette*, 21 March 1857; *Morning Chronicle*, 1 April 1857)

As doubt grew about the potential value of 'home colonies' and expensive upland improvement, from the 1860s landscapes such as Exmoor began to be appreciated for 'wildness' and their apparently uncultivated character (French 2024). By 1890, the writer J. L. Warden-Page concluded with the commonplace sentiment that:

Exmoor is best left alone: the peat and heather in hill and dale seem to defy the hand of man; and his little efforts to rob them of their natural grandeur and obdurate ruggedness are quite futile. (Warden-Page 1890: 22–3)

CONCLUSION: THE PHYSICAL LEGACIES OF IMPROVEMENT

Despite the estate's numerous misfortunes and mistakes, it was between 1844 and 1862 that modern Exmoor, as it is understood and inhabited today, was constructed materially and legally. To support his various farms, many of which still stand today, Frederic Knight also built most of the public buildings and infrastructure required to transform Simonsbath from a 'frontier settlement' into a traditional English village. In 1852, Smith convinced Knight to build a church for Exmoor to attract a 'better' quality of tenant (SHC A/EJM/1/3/7 Robert Smith to Frederic Knight, 19 March 1852). This was then joined by a village school and other amenities. The building of a church also meant the establishment of Exmoor Parish, which incorporated the Royal Forest into regional legal and political systems. By 1856, Exmoor had been 'pegged' to the Exford Petty Sessions, ensuring that its status as an area outside of the law had been firmly quashed. Although the loss of 'extra-parochial' status meant that local farmers had to pay tithes and increased taxes, the minutes of the initial Vestry Meeting show that the tenants were happy to bear these burdens now that 'poaching' and other 'criminality' amongst the local population could now be handled swiftly through 'legitimate courts' (SHC D/P/exm/9/1/1 Exmoor Vestry Minutes 1857–1946). Consequently, perhaps the greatest success of this period was the establishment of Exmoor and Simonsbath as part of regional socio-economic systems. Whilst the creation of a 'home colony' had failed, by 1862, Exmoor was far less 'distant' and 'foreign' than it had been under John Knight.

REFERENCES

DEVON HERITAGE CENTRE

262M/0/E/20/152 Fortescue of Castle Hill Estate Exmoor Estate Rentals 1864–1875; 1262M/0/E/20/153 Exmoor Estate Rentals 1875–1886.

SOMERSET HERITAGE CENTRE

A/BAZ/1/4 Draft Letter from Frederic Knight to the *Pall Mall Gazette*, c. 1880 [1883]; Tenant Contract Detailing Permanent Improvements
A/BAZ/1/5 Charles Knight to Frederic Knight, 23 October 1841.
A/BAZ/1/8 William Howchin to Frederic Knight, 16 May 1852
A/EJM/1/1/2 John Mogridge to Frederic Knight, 22 September 1846.
A/EJM/1/1/3 Frederic Knight to Lady Headley, n.d. 1852.
A/EJM/1/1/6 Frederic Knight to Jane Knight, 19 March 1841
A/EJM/1/1/6 Frederic Knight to John Knight, 25 June 1843, 13 September 1847, 28 January 1848, 13 March 1848, 15 September 1848.
A/EJM/1/1/6 Robert Smith to William Fowler, 3 November 1848.
A/EJM/1/1/6 Robert Smith to William Fowler, 3 November 1849
A/EJM/1/1/6 Rough Accounts, 29 May 1847.
A/EJM/1/1/7 John Mogridge to Frederic Knight, 24 March 1844, 26 June 1844, 22 January 1846, 30 May 1846.
A/EJM/1/3/5 Financial Statements and Accounts for Exmoor c. 1848–57
A/EJM/1/3/5 Statement of Expenditure by Tenant on the Emmett's Farm in Landlords, or Permanent, Improvement, 1849–1853.
A/EJM/1/3/6 Charles Le Blanc to Frederic Knight, 3 September 1851, 5 September 1851.
A/EJM/1/3/6 Robert Smith to Frederic Knight, 15 May 1851, 20 May 1851, 22 May 1851, 1 June 1851, 13 September 1851, 18 September 1851.
A/EJM/1/3/7 Robert Smith to Frederic Knight, 11 February 1852, 19 February 1852, 20 February 1852, 21 February 1852, 19 March 1852, 24 March 1852.
A/EJM/1/3/8 Robert Smith to Frederic Knight, 4 January 1853, 2 February 1853, 9 February 1853, 17 September 1858.
A/EJM/1/3/10 Robert Smith to Frederic Knight, 28 January 1856
A/EJM/1/3/10 Robert Smith to William Fowler, 17 April 1856.

A/EJM/1/3/11 William Fowler to Frederic Knight, 2 February 1856.

A/EJM/1/3/12 Robert Smith to Frederic Knight, 25 January 1856, 26 May 1856, 29 May 1856, 22 August 1856, 27 August 1856, 19 September 1856.

A/EJM/1/3/13 Robert Smith to Frederic Knight, 6 August 1857, 2 December 1857.

A/EJM/1/3/14 Robert Smith to Frederic Knight, 10 May 1858.

A/EJM/1/3/15 Robert Smith to Frederic Knight, 9 March 1859.

A/EJM/1/3/18 Frederick Smyth to Frederic Knight, 3 January 1868.

A/EJM/2/5/1-5 Papers Relating to Bromsgrove & Stoke Prior, Worcs., c. 1850s.

A/EJM/3/3/7 Accounts Relating to Farms and Estate Buildings on Exmoor, c. 1850s

A/EJM/6/2 Knight Estate Receivers' Accounts 1852–1862.

DD/BR/BN/31 Exmoor and Porlock Railways, 1826–1860

D/P/exm/9/1/1 Exmoor Vestry Minutes, 1857–1946

The National Archives (UK)

HO 107/617/4 1841 Census, Robert Searson, Cranmore Lodge, Deeping St. James, Bourne, Lincs.; HO 107/1330/11 1841 Census, John Bullas, High Ellers, Cantley, Doncaster; RG09/2482/15 1861 Census William Minnett, Monmouth Heath, Barkston, Newark; RG 10/4720/39 1871 Census, John Bullas, Bentinck St., Doncaster, butcher.

Newspapers

Bell's Weekly Messenger, 3 September 1849.

Daily News, 11 November 1859.

Devizes and Wiltshire Gazette, 26 June 1856.

Dorset County Chronicle, 11 September 1845, 21 September 1847

Exeter and Plymouth Gazette, 18 January 1851

Illustrated London News, 19 October 1853

Morning Chronicle, 1 April 1857.

North Devon Journal, 19 August 1847, 10 March 1853, 14 January 1858, 23 September 1858, 21 March 1861, 28 March 1861, 4 April 1861.

Oxford Chronicle and Reading Gazette, 21 March 1857

Salisbury and Winchester Journal, 25 October 1851.

Stamford Mercury, 3 February 1854.

Western Courier, 17 October 1840, 13 April 1853.

Western Times, 6 November 1841, 28 October 1848, 4 May 1850, 17 July 1852.

Primary Printed Sources

Darby, J. 1873. The Farming of Somerset. *Journal of the Bath and West of England Society* 5: 105–106.

Johnson, C. 1841. On the Improvement of Peat Soils. *Journal of the Royal Agricultural Society of England* 2: 390–400.

Pusey, P. 1841. Some Account of the Practice of English Farmers in the Improvement of Peaty Ground. *Journal of the Royal Agricultural Society of England* 2: 400–416.

———. 1843. On the Agricultural Improvements of Lincolnshire. *Journal of the Royal Agricultural Society of England* 4: 287–316.

———. 1849. The Theory and Practice of Water Meadows. *Journal of the Royal Agricultural Society of England* 10: 462–478.

Sidney, S. 1878. Exmoor Reclamation. *Journal of the Royal Agricultural Society of England* 2 (14): 72–97.

Smith, R. 1856. Bringing Moorland into Cultivation. *Journal of the Royal Agricultural Society of England* 17: 379–383.

Warden-Page, J.L. 1890. *An Exploration of Exmoor and the Hill Country of West Somerset with Some Notes on its Archaeology.* London: Seeley & Co.

Watson, J. 1845. On Reclaiming Heath Land. *Journal of the Royal Agricultural Society of England* 6: 79–101.

Secondary Works

Baker, L., F. Rowney, H. French, and R. Fyfe. 2024. Revolution and Continuity? Reassessing Nineteenth-Century Moorland Reclamation Through Palaeoecological and Historical Research. *Landscape Research* 49: 48–63. https://doi.org/10.1080/01426397.2023.2244904.

Beardmore, C. 2020. *Financing the Landed Estate: Power, Politics and People on the Marquis of Anglesey's Estate, 1812–1854.* Basingstoke: Palgrave Macmillan. https://doi.org/10.1007/978-3-030-14552-1.

Bellamy, J.M. 1962. Cotton Manufacture in Kingston Upon Hull. *Business History* 4 (2): 91–108. https://doi.org/10.1080/00076796100000035.

Biography of Gerard Spooner. https://hoaroakcottage.org/gerard-spooner/. Accessed June 19, 2024.

Bray L. S. 2010. *A Field Guide to Exmoor's Early Iron Industry.* Exmoor National Park Authority. https://www.exmoorher.co.uk/api/LibraryLink5WebService Proxy/FetchResourceFromStub/6-6-6-8-1_ec8e11d871eb2fb-66681_0 7f77559339c33d.pdf

Dezateux Robson, E. 2024. Fen Plantation: Commons, Calvinism and the Boundaries of Belonging in Early Modern England. *Journal of British Studies* 63 (1): 30–62. https://doi.org/10.1017/jbr.2023.72.

French, H. 2024. "The Wild West of England": Enclosure, Stag-Hunting, and the Creation of the New Popular Perceptions of Exmoor in the Nineteenth Century. *Cultural and Social History* 21 (4): 507–534. https://doi-org.uoelibrary.idm.oclc.org/10.1080/14780038.2024.2359502.

French, H., and L. Baker. 2023. 'The Result Never Quite Equalled the Promise': Risk, Reward, and Reclamation on Exmoor, 1840–1897. *Agricultural History Review* 71 (1): 45–65.

Orwin, C.S., and R.J. Sellick. 1970. *The Reclamation of Exmoor Forest*. David and Charles: Newton Abbot.

Pluymers, K. 2011. Taming the Wilderness in Sixteenth- and Seventeenth-Century Ireland and Virginia. *Environmental History* 16 (4): 610–632. http://www.jstor.org/stable/23049854.

Riley, H. 2019. *The Landscape of the Knights on Exmoor: A Case Study for the Exmoor Mires Partnership*. Dulverton: Exmoor Mires Project. https://doi.org/10.5284/1082836.

Williams, M. 1970. The Enclosure and Reclamation of Waste Land in England and Wales in the Eighteenth and Nineteenth Centuries. *Transactions of the Institute of Royal Geographers* 51: 55–69. https://doi.org/10.2307/621762.

Exmoor After 1860

Abstract Orwin's account focused on Robert Smith's rise and fall, and then the advent of sheep-herding. However, this chapter reveals a hidden dimension to the estate's financial recovery after 1860—the take-over of its farms by previously despised local farmers. This change contradicted the earlier 'colonising' narrative, but local farmers could make farming on Exmoor pay by drawing on familial resources and their willingness to survive on low incomes. However, the chapter shows that their tight finances were felt most by local labourers, whose living standards and opportunities were poor. It then reviews the effects of steward Frederic Smyth's new methods of land improvement, and the switch to sheep ranches on the unimproved moorland parts of the estate after 1870. By this time, however, moorland improvement was publicly depicted as an expensive failure—much to Frederic Knight's annoyance.

Keywords Agrarian history • Social history • Nineteenth-century Britain • Development • Enclosure • Moorlands • Capitalism • Rural labour • Pastoral farming • Agricultural depression

H. French et al., *The Reclamation of Exmoor Revisited*,
https://doi.org/10.1007/978-3-031-81658-1_4

THE CHANGING NARRATIVE OF IMPROVEMENT

As the previous chapter demonstrated, in the 1840s and 1850s, agrarian improvement provided the dominant theme within public discussions of Exmoor, both in terms of the strategies required to deliver it and as a moral imperative to elevate and 'civilise' the moor, its flora and fauna, and even its human inhabitants. By the end of the 1850s, local and national newspapers and publications referred repeatedly to agrarian developments such as Robert Smith's systems of drainage channels and water-meadows at his farm at Emmett's Grange, influenced in part by Smith's assiduity in promoting them (*NDJ* 15 September 1859; 21 March 1861; 20 April 1865; *Western Times* 23 December 1854; 8 October 1867).

Less was written about the area's agriculture after Smith's removal as steward in 1862 and then his departure from Exmoor six years later. Almost nothing was said about the tenanted farms that comprised half the Knight estate. Instead, observers focused on the switch to sheep herding on the in-hand portion of the estate, particularly on the prevalence of Scottish shepherds and farm hands. In October 1883, a travel-writing correspondent for the metropolitan *Pall Mall Gazette* observed that 'Scotch sheep and Scotch shepherds and Scotch collies' now comprised 'the great northern colony, both human and animal, that the proprietor of Exmoor introduced upon it some ten or a dozen years back' (*Pall Mall Gazette*, 6 October 1883). The writer thought this transplantation had succeeded because of the similarities in climate and topography (Orr 1982: 12–24; French and Baker 2023: 58–60). 'The Scotch shepherds speak most favourably of the moor as a sheepwalk; all affirm, however, that it is wetter than the proverbially wet regions from which they hail' in Perthshire and Aberdeenshire.

Other developments were also discussed as harbingers of 'civilisation' in the area, notably revived efforts to build a railway across Exmoor to Combe Martin in the mid-1860s. At the first meeting of promoters in 1866, Frederic Knight remarked that there was enough time available at Combe Martin to improve 50,000 acres (20,234 ha) encompassing 'Charles, Northmolton, Exmoor, Lynton, Brendon', which would quadruple pasture crops and lift the district out of its 'original and primitive state' (*NDJ*, 6 December 1866). Steam technology also excited one final burst of enthusiasm for agrarian improvement on Exmoor in the mid-1870s. Knight had long hoped that steam ploughing using traction engines might be powerful enough to break up the subsoil peat pan and attempted it between 1875 and 1877 (*Western Times*, 7 November 1875).

Although Orwin and Sellick quote Samuel Sidney's account of the use of the gigantic Sutherland subsoil plough on an area of deep peat at Titchcombe, the local newspapers reported an abortive, and (characteristically) fractious attempt using local machinery the previous year. Its owner, Mr Lake, claimed that Knight and his steward Frederic Smyth, had not recompensed him properly for the use and wear and tear on the machinery, and even circulated handbills to this effect. Smyth responded by decrying Lake and his machines:

> The engine was in so bad a state that it broke down before reaching Exmoor; and while under Mr. Lake's charge the body of one of the windlasses was broken on the road to Exmoor, under Mr. Lake's charge and direction, ... Ploughing began; the machinery worked very badly; ... Constant breakages occurred in all these important parts. ... Mr. Lake's tackle was so far a total failure; hardly a single continuous day's work was done, and very few acres ploughed (*NDJ*, 6 Nov. 1876).

Eventually, Knight opted for a new Barford engine, and a new steam plough, before trying the Sutherland plough on 400 acres (162 ha) of Titchcombe in the autumn of 1877, with some success (Orwin and Sellick 1970: 131).

This reignited debates about whether it was better to reclaim Exmoor, or leave it as a rare piece of wilderness in the crowded south of England. The *World* had already warned that the advent of steam ploughs on Exmoor would be 'bad news for lovers of picturesque scenery and grand views of heather-covered moorland' (quoted in *NDJ*, 21 October 1875). However, the writer was reassured by the memory 'that a predecessor of Mr. Knight's tried to cultivate the moor and was defeated with great loss'. This was too much for the *NDJ*, which revived earlier Malthusian arguments to retort that,

> ... it would be treason to higher interests to assume that in this tight little island of ours, where the soil which is to produce the food is so limited and the mouths which require it to eat are so many, it can be right to surrender to the mere purpose of recreation ... tens of thousands of acres of land, much of it cultivable with advantage, and capable of giving pasturage to sheep and cattle, and so of increasing the supplies which are to minister sustenance to the people (*NDJ*, 21 October 1875).

It reiterated that agrarian improvement was a moral duty, 'the country generally will welcome some substantial compensation in the fruits of fertility which will replenish its markets and will commend the progress of man's mission to "subdue the earth"'.

However, sustained agricultural depression in the final quarter of the nineteenth century undermined the case for large-scale reclamation projects, as the financial debacle on the Sutherland estates in Scotland showed (Simpson 2022; Tindley 2009, 2010: 34–57). Even the *North Devon Journal* was forced to admit that on Exmoor 'it would be too much to say that the changes wrought … have been all they might have been, either for the owner's profit or the public good'. In 1885, *The Leisure Hour* distilled prevailing attitudes into a single (exaggerated) reflection:

> Thousands of pounds have been spent and a thousand disappointments experienced, for Exmoor remains as it was three or four hundred years ago, a wilderness grand and lonely, with here and there a farmhouse, an orchard, or a cornfield (*The Leisure Hour*, September 1885: 629).

By the 1870s and 1880s, a new public narrative had emerged, driven in part by publication of R.D. Blackmore's *Lorna Doone*, and energetic promotion of the subscription stag-hunt on Exmoor in the national and sporting press. This emphasised the value of Exmoor's 'wildness', and depicted agriculture as a threat. In 1877, a letter to *The Times* from 'A West Countryman' complained that steam-ploughing on Exmoor would destroy one of the 'few spaces still left us in England where the weariness bred of daily toil can find refreshment' Quoted in *NDJ*, 12 September 1877).

> To the readers of 'Lorna Doone' and 'Kalterfelto' the wilds of Exmoor are very dear. Here many a toil-worn brain from Bristol, Taunton, or Exeter has been relieved by the sight of mountains clad with heather, of solitudes which, if not vast, at least afford an idea of scenes which longer purses can reach, but which bankers' clerks and ordinary tradespeople can never hope to see …

Paradoxically, therefore, the advent of mass publication and transport resulted in Exmoor being described not in terms of its untapped agrarian potential but rather of its 'unspoilt' beauty. This new narrative enticed large numbers of middle-class tourists to Ilfracombe, Linton, Lynmouth and Minehead, who also threatened to extinguish the 'wildness' of Exmoor with their own brand of intrusive modernity (French 2024).

TENANT FARMING ON EXMOOR AFTER 1860—REVERSION TO TYPE?

Even before Robert Smith's removal as steward, some rationalisation and retrenchment of the tenanted farms had occurred. This was driven, in part, by the difficulty in finding tenants for some of the more exposed and difficult farms, notably Warren Farm, Duredon and Larkbarrow. Larkbarrow was untenanted between 1852 and 1857, when it had housed labourers and miners on the estate. It was handed over to estate shepherds in 1867 (SHC A/EJM/1/3/16 William Scott to Frederic Smyth, 6 March 1867). Warren was already largely devoted to sheep production when it was divided in 1870, with the farmhouse and most of its lands transferred to the shepherds (*Bristol Mercury*, 30 April 1870; DHC Knight Estate Accounts 1262M/0/E/20/152 Mich. 1870). Duredon was taken in hand by the estate in 1868 (SHC A/EJM/1/3/18 Frederic Smyth to Frederic Knight, 3 May 1868). This trend continued through the 1870s, with Pinkery farmhouse and lands being occupied by shepherds from 1875, Winstitchen farm (split from Honeymead in 1862) handed over to shepherds in 1878, and Wintershead in 1885 (DHC Knight Estate Accounts 1262M/0/E/20/152 Mich. 1873 Pinkery; Tait Little Diary vol. 5, 1878, Winstitchen; Tait Little Diary vol. 4, 1885, Wintershead). Shepherds had also been based at Ricksy Ball since 1860, when it had been divided from Cornham Farm (TNA RG9/1607 Exmoor Census Return 1861). There are significant fluctuations in the figures for acreages let and in-hand recorded in the Knight estate rentals, but it appears that the acreage occupied by tenants fell from 9500 acres (3844 ha) in 1852 to 7700 acres (3116 ha) in the late 1850s and settled at 6800 acres (2752 ha) in the late 1870s, before falling to 5500 acres (2226 ha) in the mid-1880s. If the remainder was in hand, the amount of the Exmoor estate retained by Frederic Knight rose from 7000 acres (2833 ha) in 1852 to 12,000 acres (4856 ha) in the 1880s. As Burton suggests, although some of the pastures around the former farmhouses at Simonsbath and Winstitchen had been improved, most of the in-hand estate was unimproved moorland (Burton 1989: 103).

In addition, from the mid-1850s, Smith split off 'allotments' from some of the farms, carved others directly out of the moors, and let them on a short-term basis to locals (*Dorset County Chronicle*, 14 December 1854). Approximately 10 such 'farm' allotments were created, although their flexible and temporary nature meant that the acreages quoted varied considerably from rental to rental. Crooked Post seems to have had at least two allotments of 56 ac and 36 acres (23 and 15 ha) respectively (DHC 1262M/0/E/20/152 Knight Estate Accounts 1857, 1864 and 1870; DHC 1262M/0/E/20/153, 1873, 1875, 1876 and 1877). There were larger allotments at Long Holcombe: 'Middle Long Holcombe allotment' was 414 acres (168 ha), while there were at least two at 'Eastern Long Holcombe', of 212 and 15 acres (86 and 6 ha), respectively. There were at least four allotments at Great and Little Ashcombe, all under 100 acres (40 ha), and at least two at Ricksy Ball. Such unimproved land provided relatively cheap summer grazing, and in 1880, Frederic Knight claimed that these allotments had provided a 'farming ladder' up which several local labourers and farmers' sons had climbed to occupy more substantial tenancies. He named 16 tenants 'paying me together the annual sum of £1,270' and claimed that they 'were all of them within my recollection agricultural labourers, excepting two whose fathers rose from the ranks' (Orwin and Sellick 1970: 116). Their rents ranged between £17 and £200, with 12 paying less than £100 per annum, for farms of 50–400 acres (20–162 ha) (DHC 1262M/0/E/20/153 Knight Estate Accounts 1880).

The estate provided other opportunities, because it also recruited some relatively young tenants. 27 leases were granted to tenants aged under 30 years. Most were for cottage properties, but 13 were for farm-sized holdings. Many of these were to the sons (or in one case the daughter) of local farming families, often to pairs of unmarried brothers (TNA HO 107/1890/361 1851 Census Ellen Blake, daughter of John Blake). So, in 1867, 29-year-old John Rudd and his 23-year-old brother George took on the lease of a portion of Honeymead Farm. They were sons of John Rudd, who had been farming 125 acres (51 ha) at Charles in South Molton, Devon in 1851 (TNA HO 107/1891 1851 Census, John Rudd Sr.). In 1852, 26-year-old Thomas Crick rented 170 acres (69 ha) in Warren Allotment, and later went on to rent Warren Farm. He and his brother Richard (who later assisted him at Warren Farm) were sons of Thomas Crick of Boomham Farm, Porlock (TNA HO 107/936/10 1841 Census, Thomas Crick Sr.). Similarly, 29-year-old John Crang, who rented 400 acres (162 ha) of Titchcombe allotment in 1872 was the son of William Crang who farmed 700 acres (283 ha) at Challacombe (TNA HO 107/1892/387 1851 Census, William Crang Sr.). He farmed on Exmoor before taking over his father's farm in the early 1880s (TNA RG 11/2245/24 1881 Census, John Crang). By that time, such tenants were sometimes the sons of Exmoor farmers. Albert Richards took over Horsen Farm (763 acres/309 ha) aged 28 in 1882 but was the son of George Richards, who had farmed Wintershead from 1859 until his death in 1878 (TNA RG 10/2180/13 1871 Census, George Richards). Although the ages given in census enumerators' returns are notoriously rounded, these age ranges are significant, because in most censuses, those described as farmers (i.e., household heads) were much older. In Lincolnshire, Mills observed that farmers had an average age of 50.6 years, 'since only older men would have the capital and experience required for running a farm' on the Lincolnshire heaths (Mills and Mills 1997: 142). Mills notes that farm bailiffs (managers) tended to be younger, but the distribution on Exmoor implies that it was easier for farmers' sons in their late 20s or early 30s to gain their first tenancy on the Knight estate, instead of serving as a cowman or bailiff elsewhere.

A new estate steward, Frederic Smyth arrived in 1866 and implemented a scheme for developing peatland soils across the in-hand portions of the estate by planting successive rapeseed crops and then grazing sheep. This echoed the Sutherland reclamations, in which pastures were improved to support flocks all year round, to capitalise on the buoyant mutton and wool prices of the mid-1860s. Ironically, though, in the same way that the acquisition of Exmoor by John Knight missed the peak of upland enclosure during the Napoleonic war, and Frederic Knight's experiments in 'high farming' only got under way after the repeal of the Corn Laws, the shift to sheep farming only caught the tail-end of the mid-Victorian expansion in sheep numbers. These rose rapidly in sheep-corn regions into the 1870s, as farmers attempted to maintain their incomes by moving more towards livestock/wool production than grain, spurred by an expanding mechanised West Yorkshire woollen industry and rising domestic demand for mutton. However, sheep numbers peaked in England and Wales in 1872, at 19.9 million, five years after the Knight and Frederic Smyth moved decisively into sheep ranching (Collins 2000: 39). Stock prices for sheep peaked in 1883 but declined by approximately 30 per cent into the mid-1890s, as competition began from imports of frozen carcases from Australia and New Zealand. Similarly, wool prices were at their highest in the mid-1860s but declined relentlessly thereafter, to a low point in 1903 (Orr 1982: 21–3; Robinson 1988: 33). In 1882, the Royal Commission on Agriculture found that in North Devon the low prices for sheep in 1879 'frightened men for a time, and the price of wool has for some time been disheartening' but claimed that the situation had stabilised (UKPP

C.3375 Royal Commission on Agriculture 1882: 33). Sheep-producing regions, including North Devon, suffered from the large-scale outbreak of scab, liver rot and liver fluke between 1878 and 1882, when the national flock declined from 18.9 million to 14.9 million (Robinson 1988: 33). In 1883, Knight crossed swords with the *Pall Mall Gazette*'s correspondent about the health of local sheep, stating emphatically that 'No sheep with liver rot, or fluke, has ever been known on Exmoor, and none with foot-and-mouth disease for a quarter of a century' (*Pall Mall Gazette*, 24 Oct. 1883). This drew a response from Robert Smith's son that sheep on Exmoor may not have had liver fluke but did suffer from scab—an intervention prompted in part by Knight's aside that he had only had an 'honest steward' on Exmoor since Smith Sr's departure (*Pall Mall Gazette*, 26 Oct. 1883). Certainly, the estate may have benefitted by selling store lambs to lowland farmers desperate to re-stock.

Frederic Smyth's new methods coincided with the advent of the MAFF 68 'June Returns' in 1866. Tables 1 and 2 illustrate the relative changes in arable and livestock production on Exmoor, compared to five surrounding parishes. They are indexed against figures for 1882, selected as a midpoint in the series, and a year in which figures were available for all the sample parishes. While the figures aggregate the tenant farms and the in-hand sheep ranches on Exmoor, they reveal that (in some respects) the cultivation of Exmoor was converging with the more mature patterns in neighbouring parishes. There were much larger absolute declines in the acreages of wheat, barley and oats produced on Exmoor than in other parishes, as wheat prices collapsed and as self-sufficiency (particularly for livestock feed) became less important. Similarly, Table 2 demonstrates that the numbers of sheep on Exmoor rose faster than those in other parishes. Since Exmoor was three to four times larger than any of its neighbours, this represented a significant increase in absolute numbers, from 8–9000 per annum in the late 1860s to over 17,000 in the final years of the nineteenth century.

Table 2 shows that the numbers of other livestock remained stable across the period, apart from a doubling in the number of horses and Exmoor ponies kept in Hawkridge (from c. 50 in the late 1860s to over 100 in the late 1890s). The 1882 Royal Agricultural Commission report on North Devon noted that oil-seed rape was cultivated specifically as part of a regime of peatland reclamation to create improved grasslands (UKPP C.3375 Royal Commission on Agriculture 1882: 33). It noted that Smyth ensured that the land was first pared and burned (ashes were ploughed

Table 1 Relative changes in arable cropped acreages on Exmoor and in surrounding parishes in MAFF68 Reports, where 1882=100

Parishes	Wheat and barley		Oats		Oil-seed rape		Turnips	
	1866–1879	1885–1901	1866–1879	1885–1901	1866–1879	1885–1901	1866–1879	1885–1901
Exmoor	346.2	24.5	130.1	95.8	86.1	86.4	202.8	105.6
Dulverton	138.4	64.4	103.7	111.8	98.9	87.7	116.4	93.2
Exford	120.7	44.9	110.2	109.7	88.0	216.5	131.5	112.6
Hawkridge	89.1	62.8	100.2	101.6	86.7	72.4	100.5	110.5
Luccombe	93.0	51.2	76.3	81.9	62.5	115.2	92.1	67.6
Withypool	167.7	95.1	101.3	94.0	104.0	172.0	119.0	101.1

Table 2 Relative changes in livestock numbers on Exmoor and in surrounding parishes in MAFF68 Reports, where 1882=100

	Horses		Cattle		Sheep	
Parishes	1866–1879	1885–1901	1866–1879	1885–1901	1866–1879	1885–1901
Exmoor	79.3	98.8	100.4	99.1	76.0	110.1
Dulverton	82.5	97.0	88.8	102.2	94.9	103.8
Exford	87.4	89.9	82.3	92.6	98.6	99.5
Hawkridge	54.8	115.8	97.7	98.7	97.6	100.8
Luccombe	87.4	70.8	65.8	98.6	103.9	92.3
Withypool	89.4	130.0	111.3	117.7	118.6	104.4

Table 3 Estimated acreages of rape-seed cultivation from MAFF68 Reports, as a proxy for land improvement, 1866–1901

Parish	Total rape Ac.	% Total years recorded	Total rape Ac. (incl. missing yrs.)	Divided by 3	'Improved' Ac. as % total land area
Exmoor	6921.8	80.0	8306.2	2768.7	13.6
Dulverton	2308.5	51.4	3429.8	1143.3	13.1
Exford	2208.8	62.9	3029.1	1009.7	17.0
Hawkridge	1045.0	65.7	1403.3	467.8	13.8
Luccombe	116.8	45.7	180.1	60.0	1.5
Withypool	854.8	62.9	1172.2	390.7	10.0

into the soil), then limed at the rate of three tonnes per acre. Rape seed was sown on the land for three or four years consecutively, on which sheep were fed. The rapeseed roots would break up the peat pan, after which the land could be ploughed and used as improved grassland. Consequently, the acreages of rapeseed reported in the MAFF68 returns provide a proxy for the total area of grassland improved on Exmoor and surrounding parishes. There are missing years for each parish in this MAFF68 series, but if the area planted with rapeseed was similar in the missing years, we can estimate the total acreage reclaimed. Given that rape was grown in a three- or four-year planting cycle, the total acreage should be divided by three (at least) to get a figure for the net land area improved—as shown in Table 3. These figures suggest that the area of improved grazing on Exmoor increased from c. 3500 acres (1416 ha) in the early 1870s to c. 6300 acres (2549 ha) in the late 1890s, out of 22,000 acres (8903 ha) in total on the

Knight estate. The figure for Exmoor is much larger than for neighbouring parishes, because Exmoor Parish was much bigger. However, the proportion of the land area developed by rapeseed on Exmoor resembled that in surrounding parishes and is consistent with the reported area of improved grassland.

This area is consistent with the relatively concentrated zone of 'improved pastures' in the centre of Exmoor plotted on the 1935 Land Utilisation survey (Dudley Stamp 1941: 517), shown in Fig. 3, Chapter "Polemics and Practices". These were pastures formed a wedge tapering westwards from the extensive 'old' improvements around Exford and narrowing along the Simonsbath road to include Honeymead, Simonsbath, Duredon, Cornham and Driver farms. There were also significant areas of improved pasture in the south forest, surrounding Emmett's Grange, and its neighbours, Wintershead and Horsen. Individual fields of improved grassland surrounded Tom's Hill, Larkbarrow, Picked Stones, and Sherdon and Lower Sherdon farms. In total, approximately 6000 acres (2428 ha) had been subject to some improvement by the 1890s, ranging from simple drainage channels to Frederic Smyth's elaborate regime of paring, burning, liming, and rape cultivation. Another 8000 acres (3237 ha) on the table lands in the northern forest remained entirely unenclosed and unimproved. Unsurprisingly, therefore, reclamation efforts were most successful and extensive where they were most sustained, on the farms that had remained in the hands of tenants through the period—Honeymead, Simonsbath, Duredon, Cornham, Driver and Emmett's. On the less attractive farms that quickly became sheep herdings, any 'improvements' were a residual legacy of the faltering efforts of tenants in the early 1850s. Widespread drainage efforts in the North Forest and west of Simonsbath did not create improved pastures, because they were not sustained, nor were they integrated into the more intensive systems of rape and 'artificial' grass seeds practiced around the tenanted farms. The estate's later sheep herdings were an extensive, low-cost method of extracting a return from largely unimproved grass and moorland.

FARMERS AND LABOURERS

In 1929, Orwin described the tenant farmers of Exmoor as 'almost a hereditary class, and fully 75 per cent of them began at the bottom of the ladder, or at one generation from it', and stressed the importance of families as sources of connections, support and capital (Orwin and Sellick

1970: 143). The records of the Hayes family typify this experience and illustrate the strategies adopted by these local families, as they branched out onto Exmoor. The family combined a holding outside the estate with renting a farm and allotments from the Knights. William Hayes (b. 1816) rented Coombe Farm in Exford and Lower Pitsworthy in the period between the 1840s and the 1870s, giving him around 720 acres (291 ha) (SHC A/DVF/1/5 Accounts of George and William Hayes, 11 vols., 1862–1914; TNA RG 10/2358/5 1871 Census, William Hayes). He also rented allotments on Exmoor, from the Knights and others, and a portion of Warren Farm on the Knight estate in the 1870s. His sons John and James took over after his death in 1876, assisting their mother Charity, and James Hayes kept some succinct accounts which cover Coombe and Lower Pitsworthy and some Exmoor allotments between 1881 and 1887 (SHC A/DVF/1/3 Accounts of James Hayes, 1879–1888; TNA RG 11/2358/80 1881 Census, Charity Hayes).

He rented 710 acres (287 ha) in total, at about 10s. per acre—approximately 15 per cent of it from Frederic Knight. Like other local farmers, James benefitted both from the family infrastructure of equipment, know-how and contacts but also from its circulating capital, notably the £102 borrowed from a 'Miss Hayes' (his sister?) at the start of his tenancy. Such capital transfers within families were common among Exmoor tenant farmers. In 1887, James Buckingham got into financial difficulties and exposed a web of local credit relations. Buckingham had farmed allotments rented from the Knight estate. In 1880, he had been loaned £100 by another farmer, for whom George Brook had provided security (who farmed 180 acres (73 ha) at Sherdon next to the Exmoor estate). After Buckingham became insolvent, Brook became liable for the debt but refused to pay (*EPG*, 15 June 1889). At the same time, Buckingham's nephew, George Stinner, a small farmer, had lost his farm to the mortgagee but was accused of concealing assets by selling some of his livestock to his uncle for cash (*Western Times*, 15 February 1889). Clearly, family members drew on this web of connections for start-up capital, loans, stock and equipment, in ways that obscured legal liability, but also gave them a comparative advantage over outsiders for whom such resources were not so immediately available.

Each year James Hayes sold about 140–150 sheep, 12–15 bullocks or steers, 4–6 Exmoor ponies, as well as wool. In many respects, his farm resembles one from the seventeenth century, because he aimed for self-sufficiency, growing oats and selling butter, ducks, geese and eggs. The

1882 Royal Commission report noted that tenants 'persist in attempting to grow enough Wheat for their own household consumption, there being evidently a strong feeling among the smaller men against *buying* anything' (UKPP C.3375 Royal Commission on Agriculture 1882: 33).

Hayes did spend money on improving grassland, primarily on the Exmoor allotments, but generally only on relatively small plots (totalling just 50 acres/20 ha), and not by using lime in the quantities recommended by the Knight estate. Only on the smallest plot of just over an acre did he reach their three tonnes target. Presumably, he did what he could afford, but he could not afford to do very much, because his net profits were very small. The figure varied considerably from year to year, being highest when he sold three years' worth of wool in 1885 for £294, and negative in the first two years of his tenure. The average net profit between 1881 and 1887 was just £45 per annum, under £1 per week. Given that he grew most of his own food, this money represented 'cash at the bank (or money under the bed)', but only a six or seven per cent return on his turnover (Hoyle 2016: 35). Hayes was in his early thirties without grown-up children to assist him, so his labour costs of £40–50 per annum were probably higher than for an older tenant. A breach-of-promise case involving Henry Tucker, aged 27, son of the tenant of Emmett's Grange Farm in 1889 revealed that despite claiming to his jilted fiancée that 'he was worth £500', he admitted in court that his mother held the lease, and 'he and his brother managed the farm for her, receiving no pay, but their board, clothing, and pocket money', plus £92 he had inherited from his father (*Western Morning News,* 23 July 1889). The expectation on Exmoor seems to have been that family members would not receive wages, just their subsistence out of the produce of the farm.

Hayes' experiences echoed the Royal Commission on Agriculture findings in the region in the period. The 1894 Commission gave the example of a farmer in Barnstaple Union, whose land was probably of much better quality than Hayes' (UKPP C.7728 Royal Commission on Agriculture Report 1895, Appendix C II: 54). The farmer possessed 54 acres (22 ha) of wheat, 25 acres (10 ha) of oats, 4 acres (1.6 ha) of barley, and 30 acres (12 ha) of turnips. He had a stock of 400 sheep (c. 190 ewes, 210 lambs), 70 cattle, 16 horses and poultry. This provided him with a much larger turnover than Hayes, £2410 in 1892, and £1615 in 1893. Across the two years, his total profit was £105 (with a loss in 1893), which averaged out at £52 per annum, or £1 per week. This reflected the sustained drop in stock prices and wool which were 25–40 per cent lower than in the late 1870s in North Devon, which fared better than other parts of the country.

Such adverse economic conditions put further emphasis on the importance of family networks, both in supporting farmers financially in years of repeated losses and marginal profits, and perhaps also in trapping children into a parsimonious existence that outsiders now chose to avoid. Much of the cost of farming on such tight margins was borne by the labourers. Although John Knight had to pay higher wages to attract labourers to dig drains and build roads in the 1820s and 1830s, 30 years later, wage rates on Exmoor resembled those elsewhere, even if there may have been more opportunities for live-in service (driven by the lack of housing). Most of the evidence about labourers' lives in this period comes from the Petty Sessions records of Barnstaple and South Molton, so it must be read 'against the grain' to counter its inbuilt social and legal biases. Unsurprisingly, the most common offences were petty theft and drunkenness. The theft of food or foodstuffs was reported relatively often. In February 1859, 53-year-old Samuel Harris was convicted of stealing three bushels of oats and two of wheat from his employer, George Avery Gould, of Simonsbath Barton Farm (*TCWA*, 2 February, 30 March 1859). Harris had previous convictions and may have been taking the grain to feed his family, who were evicted by Gould from a tied cottage in Simonsbath four months later (*TCWA*, 8 June 1859). The following year, James Frayen of Simonsbath was convicted of stealing bacon from a joint hanging in the kitchen of the village inn, where he had been drinking (*TCWA*, 11 April 1860). The innkeeper, Samuel Gifford, had been on the alert because the joint had 'been cut on previous occasions'. Other thefts by itinerant traders were reported, from houses left unoccupied (but not unmonitored), or of livestock on Exmoor (*TCWA*, 30 October 1861; *Express and Echo*, 20 June 1879; *NDJ*, 4 September 1884; *WSFP*, 23 October 1886).

Some thefts and other incidents appear to have been disputes over wages, or because of labourers being dismissed or leaving service on farms. Thomas Kidwell, a 21-year-old labourer, was charged with stealing from Emmett's Grange farmhouse in Feb. 1881. Kidwell had previously been employed by the tenant, Mrs Tucker, and was charged with breaking in and stealing a 'loaf of bread value 10d, pound of butter, value 1s 6d, and other articles', plus a pair of boots from one of the other servants. Presumably, Kidwell intended to use these items to make his way off the moor. Personal animus by former employees could also result in threats or actual cases of arson (*TCWA*, 13 July 1870). Some farmers, such as John

Blake, also accumulated a long track record of aggression (*NDJ*, 15 January 1857, *TCWA*, 31 July 1861, 2 April 1862, 2 September 1863). In 1893, the Suffolk labourer George Jones was acquitted at the Assizes of a charge of arson against George Richards of Horsen Farm. Jones had worked for Richards on the farm for four years, before leaving abruptly in 1891 (*NDJ*, 14 September 1893; *WSFP*, 16 September 1893). Richards had refused to return several items of clothing that Jones had left behind, or to pay him the residue of a month's wages. Jones was alleged to have replied 'It won't do you any good', before leaving. That night, a corn rick on the farm had been set alight, but the evidence against Jones was circumstantial, and there were procedural irregularities by the magistrates (*Western Daily Press*, 3 November 1893). Previously, George Richards had lost a case against an indoor farm-servant, Richard Gubb, for leaving before the end of his annual contract, because the agreement had been purely verbal (*WSFP*, 12 January 1884). Gubb had agreed to work for him for £14 per annum. Although board and lodging had been provided, the wage rate worked out at only 5*s* 9*d* per week.

Although a church was built in Simonsbath in 1856, and the village acquired a school, and (eventually) such late-Victorian staples as a hotel, a cricket team and concert parties, the main focal points for labourers were its four inns—the Simonsbath Inn; Gallon House/Red Deer Inn on the road between Simonsbath and Exford, the Acland Arms at Moles Chamber, and the Sportsman's Inn at Sandyway. These remained places of sociability for labourers, and sites of interest to police and magistrates, even if they were probably less frequented than in periods when Exmoor contained mobile, rootless populations of Irish labourers in John Knight's time, or Cornish and Welsh miners in the explorations of the 1850s. John Buckingham, who kept the Sportsman in the 1870s, acquired a reputation for lawlessness—notably violence against his customers, irregular opening hours and handling stolen goods (*TCWA*, 6 September 1871; *WSFP*, 10 December 1881; *Express and Echo*, 20 June 1879). This led to local objections to the renewal of his licence (*WSFP*, 27 Aug. 1881). There were similar complaints of drunkenness at the Red Deer Inn (*TCWA*, 3rd October 1866; *WSFP*, 4 September 1880).

Inevitably, in the absence of other opportunities, drunkenness was the main recreational activity available for many labourers. The most infamous instance of this was the 1858 case of the Exmoor murderer, William Burgess, a widower who lodged in crowded accommodation next to Gallon House, and admitted killing his daughter Anna-Maria, apparently so that he could spend the 2s 6d per week maintenance money on drink instead (*NDJ*, 13 January 1859). There were frequent press reports of Exmoor labourers found drunk and incapable in the streets, sometimes repeatedly, and the accidental death of Northumbrian shepherd Adam Dunn, gives a brief insight into the sociability available in local inns (*NDJ*, 14 May 1863, 4 November 1875; *WSFP*, 9 September 1876; *NDJ*, 8 July 1880; *WSFP*, 4 December 1880; *NDJ*, 13 March 1884; Burton 1989: 114–5). Dunn lived at the Larkbarrow Farm herding with his brother William. He had been found unconscious, leaning against a hedge on his way back to the farmhouse, and died the following day. The night before, he had been at the Acland Arms, playing the fiddle at a dance. He left at 9 pm to walk the six miles back to Larkbarrow, having purchased a gallon of whisky. The verdict was given as 'exposure'. There were also incidents in which some of the tenant farmers had been apprehended for being drunk in the highway (*EPG*, 10 March 1891; *NDJ*, 8 May 1895; *EPG*, 14 August 1895). Drink was an essential accompaniment to male social gatherings, from auctions to hunting, and public houses provided an escape from the isolation, monotony and often cramped living conditions in farm garrets, and overcrowded cottages across the moor (*TCWA*, 3 October 1866). It also contributed to the undercurrent of domestic and public violence within these dense rural social networks.

MANAGING THE 'IN-HAND' ESTATE: THE SCOTTISH SHEPHERDS

For observers, after 1860, the main developments on Exmoor were the switch to sheep herding on the 'in-hand' half of the estate, and the prevalence of Scottish shepherds and farm hands. As we have seen, the advent of this 'great northern colony' captured the attention of the *Pall Mall Gazette's* reporter in 1883. Along with imported Scottish Cheviots and Blackface sheep (improved breeds that combined meat and wool production, with the ability of traditional breeds to survive in harsh upland terrains), Frederic Smyth also recruited 18 Scots labourers and 3 from Northumbria, who accompanied the sheep and settled on Exmoor, at rates of pay that were higher than those offered to local labourers (Brassley 2000: 557–8; Burton 1989: 121). Smyth also tried (unsuccessfully) to recruit several Scottish farmers as tenants on Exmoor (Orwin and Sellick 1970: 115–29; Burton 1989: 112–30).

As with the recruitment drive in previous decades, during the 1860s, advertisements were posted in the 'border papers' to encourage men to 'go south' by offering 'Large Tracts of Excellent Sheep Land to Suit Applicants from this Region' (SHC A/EJM/1/3/18 J.W. MacDonald to Frederic Knight, 20 June 1868). Once again, the men from Scotland were presented as being superior in knowledge, skill and temperament to the 'native' population of Exmoor. In 1868, the estate's steward, Frederic Smyth, described two potential Scottish tenants as 'very fine specimens of the "genus homo"' and 'thorough men of business' who would be able to improve the land 'in a broad scale more than any man here' as the locals 'do not think it possible without a considerable outlay' (SHC A/ EJM/1/3/18 Frederic Smyth to Frederic Knight, 3 January 1868, 6 January 1868). Indeed, the estate's agents became so enamoured with Scottish 'talent' that it often became their sole priority during periods of mass hiring.

One of these new recruits was Robert Tait Little, a shepherd from Dumfriesshire, who arrived in Exmoor in the late 1860s. He was promoted to head shepherd in the estate in 1876 and, from then until his death in 1907, kept detailed annual records of the sheep on the eight original herdings, Badgeworthy, Cornham, Duredon, Hoar Oak/The Chains, Larkbarrow, Pinkery, Simonsbath, and Winstitchen, to which Honeymead and Wintershead were added during the period. As Fig. 1 shows, the number of sheep on the estate herdings increased from just over 8000 in the late 1870s to a peak of 11,000 in the years immediately

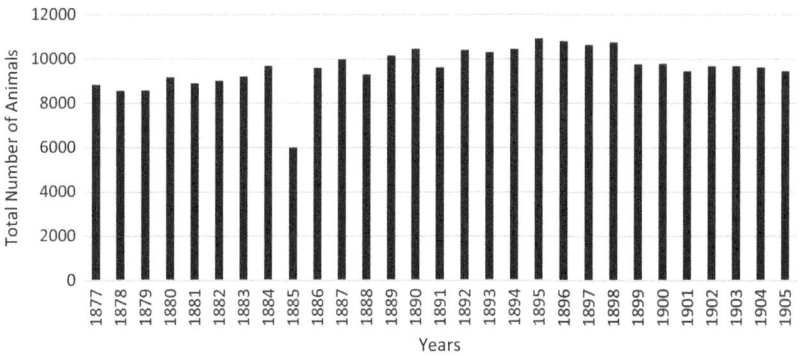

Fig. 1   Total number of ewes and lambs on ten in-hand sheep herdings, Knight estate, Exmoor, 1877–1905

preceding Frederic Knight's death in 1897 (DHC 1262M/0/E/21/7 & 8, Robert Tait Little Sheep Diaries, 1876–1907). Unsurprisingly, as Table 4 shows, it was easier to look after sheep on the lower, more sheltered herdings south of Simonsbath (such as Wintershead, Simonsbath and Cornham) than on those on the exposed plateau of 'table lands' north of the village (notably Larkbarrow, Badgeworthy and Hoar Oak/Chains). The estate's herd comprised almost two-thirds of all the sheep pastured on Exmoor in these years, and lamb sales provided most of the income. Culled ewes, fat lambs and hoggs not selected for breeding were sold off in September and October, to reduce the numbers required to over-winter. Young ewes were often protected by being wintered on lowlands outside the estate, including Ilfracombe, Combe Martin and Cadeleigh near Tiverton (Burton 1989: 123). Each year, Tait Little sold approximately 10–15 per cent of his breeding stock and two-thirds of the lambs. In 1877, Tait Little noted that of a flock of 8163 animals, 3067 had been sold, of which 2444 were that year's lambs (Tait Little, Diary, vol. 5: 19–22).

Such precautions were necessary, because Tait Little recorded that late winter snows in March 1878 trapped 790 sheep, of which 290 died, particularly on Larkbarrow and Badgeworthy (Tait Little, Diary, vol. 1: 29). At Duredon in January 1881, he recorded five successive days with between 12 and 22 degrees of frost (temperatures below freezing) (Tait Little, Diary, vol. 1: 67). Such temperatures tended to belie Frederic Knight's assertion that 'shepherds from the Scotch borders have frequently remarked, on receiving accounts of snowstorms in their native hills, that on coming to Exmoor they had come into the land of Goshen' (*Pall Mall Gazette*, 24 Oct. 1883). High levels of stock mortality occurred across the estate in the winters of 1877, 1878, 1885–1888, particularly in 1890, 1891–1893 and again in 1896. Over 200 sheep died at Larkbarrow in 1890 and 1892, and over 100 at Badgeworthy in 1877, 1878, 1886, 1892, 1896 and 1904. After 1878, the estate built circular stone shielings at Badgeworthy, Hoar Oak and The Chains, on the Scottish model, to offer some protection to sheep left out on the higher grounds, but the acute winters of the final quarter of the century were tough on shepherds and sheep (Burton 1989: 120; Hegarty and Wilson-North 2014: 49).

While Frederic Knight assured the estate's eventual purchaser, Lord Fortescue, that it generated £9–11,000 per annum by this time, other figures put the total income at around £8,500 (DHC1262M/0/E/5/3 Correspondence about Exmoor estate sale 1885–1886). The estate rents

Table 4 Mortality levels for sheep on Exmoor herdings, percentage of annual flock per herding, 1877–1905

Herding	1877–1879	1880–1884	1885–1889	1890–1894	1895–1899	1900–1905	Mean
Winstitchen	4.7	1.8	3.4	2.3	2.9	2.4	2.9
Simonsbath	3.5	1.8	4.1	3.5	3.0	2.3	3.0
Larkbarrow	7.0	5.6	6.7	9.6	4.6	2.7	6.0
Badgeworthy	8.1	4.8	7.0	6.4	6.9	5.5	6.4
Hoar Oak/The Chains	5.4	5.5	7.3	6.0	5.9	4.7	5.8
Cornham	5.6	2.2	4.2	2.2	1.2	0.0	2.6
Duredon	5.3	3.7	4.5	2.9	2.5	2.3	3.6
Pinkery	5.5	2.4	5.8	2.9	3.5	3.1	3.9
Wintershead	0.0	0.3	3.1	1.7	2.1	0.3	1.3

provided a net yield of about £3,000 per annum, so it is likely that the sheep herdings generated most of the estate's income (DHC 1262M/0/E/20/152 & 153 Knight Estate Accounts, 1864–1885). This may explain both why the Knight estate continued to expand its sheep flocks into the 1890s, in the face of falling prices, and why the policy was partially reversed under Lord Fortescue, whose much larger estates provided a better rental income. However, the fact that Fortescue was quick to turn Larkbarrow (the most exposed herding) into a hunting and shooting let also implies that Frederic Knight may have been resistant to the recreational management of uplands that was spreading rapidly in Scotland (Orr 1982).

RECRUITMENT AND EXPERIENCE

Contrary to the image presented of Scottish shepherds in the correspondence of Frederic Knight, from the census records and other official documents, it appears that many of the men recruited for Exmoor were not experts in sheep rearing but normal farm labourers who had worked a variety of jobs before they found themselves employed by the Knights. Although many had been shepherds in Scotland prior to responding to the estate's advertisements in the Scottish newspapers, very few of them were Highlanders. While men such as Peter Murray, William Scott, John Gourdie and James Johnstone had been shepherds (or in Scott's case a bailiff) on farms surpassing 1000 acres (405 ha), the rest had spent their lives working on farms ranging from 200 to 500 acres (81 to 202 ha) (SNA 772/1/2 1871 Census, Peter Murray; SNA 067/2/4 1851 Census, William Scott; SNA 634/1/10 1871 Census, John Gourdie; SNA 607/6/7 1871 Census, James Johnstone). These farms were similar in size to those in and around Exmoor, so these Scottish migrants did not necessarily have more of an affinity with large sheep farms than local shepherds.

Some of the names and locations that recur in the trajectories of these shepherds indicate how Frederic Knight recruited these men. Several worked at Auldhouseburn Farm, at Muirkirk in Ayrshire, a nationally renowned breeder of Scottish Blackface sheep (Hide 2013). Knight also used local dealers as intermediaries: J. W. MacDonald, the Knight family's sheep dealer in Scotland, approached David Bryden to recruit him (A/ EJM/1/3/16 J. W. MacDonald to Frederic Knight, 17 June 1867). Similarly, immediately prior to arriving on Exmoor, Thomas Graham worked for a cattle dealer, specialising in the breed of cattle that the Knights favoured (SNA 772/1/2 1871 Census, Thomas Graham). The proximity of these men to the Knight family's network of agents and dealers in Scotland drew them into the employ of Frederic Knight.

Most of the men recruited for Exmoor were from lowland counties, particularly Dumfriesshire, Lanarkshire, Kirkcudbrightshire and Ayrshire. Frederic Knight's surviving correspondence suggests that he purchased most of his Scottish sheep from the fairs in these counties, so he had probably amassed many contacts in the region. For example, William Davidson was employed by Frederic Knight after having been assigned to drive Blackface sheep down to Exmoor (DHC 2579A/PR/1/15 Lynton Parish Marriage Register, 8 October 1870). A transfer of livestock, therefore, came with a direct transfer of personnel, and knowledge.

However, word-of-mouth remained the most successful advertising tool for both local and Scottish shepherds. Critically, it led to the recruitment of the 'Four [Scots] Cousins' (John Renwick, William Johnstone, James Johnstone and William Davidson), who became a foundation for shepherding at Hoar Oak and Badgworthy throughout the 1870s and 1880s (http://www.peasantstopuddles.org/cousins.htm). Similarly, the Murray brothers and the Little brothers established themselves, successively, at Toms Hill and Larkbarrow herdings. Although some of these men did not last long on Exmoor, the evidence suggests that Scottish shepherds established a pattern of chain-migration that 'pulled' family members down to Exmoor.

SUCCESSES, FAILURES AND TRANSIENCE

As with the tenant farmers analysed above, so the shepherds who arrived on Exmoor can be divided into 'successes' and 'failures'. The former included William Little, Thomas Graham or John Gourdie who used their time on Exmoor to save up money and then purchase farmsteads (after the Exmoor estate was taken over by the Fortescue family in 1898) (Burton 1989: 191, 227; http://hoaroakcottage.org/2017/10/11/grahams/; *Western Times*, 1 October 1920). Indeed, by the time of his death in 1931, after 50 years on Exmoor, Gourdie had amassed a small fortune of £20,000 (Burton 1989: 191). Many of their descendants continued to be central to the agricultural life of the region into the late twentieth century. Equally, there were a few men struggling for work in Scotland who managed to find some employment in Exmoor. Donald MacDougal, for instance, was unmarried and out of permanent employment in Scotland before deciding to take a chance on Exmoor, where he became one of the estate's longest-serving shepherds (Burton 1989: 117).

Yet, the successes of a half-dozen men are matched by the abject failure of others. Their experiences mirrored those of the tenant farmers: when things went wrong for the Scottish shepherds on Exmoor, it was a complete disaster. The most dramatic was John Renwick, who was committed to a mental asylum after eight years on Exmoor (Tait Little, Stock Diary vol. 3: 27; https://www.scottishindexes.com/hentry.aspx?hid=648001). Similarly, Peter Murray was dismissed and imprisoned briefly for stealing sheep, although this did not impact his long-term employability as a shepherd in Scotland (*WSFP*, 8 October 1892; Tait Little, Stock Diary vol. 4: 9–10). However, most of these Scottish shepherds had a 'neutral' or 'transient' experience of Exmoor. Nine of the 19 stayed for less than 10 years, and they soon found themselves back in Scotland with another job, often landing a position unrelated to sheep farming. Unlike the tenant farmers, whose sunk costs tied them to the estate, as waged workers, the Scottish shepherds simply left when prospects declined for them on Exmoor.

Significantly, perhaps, in the late nineteenth century, every Scottish shepherd traced worked for the estate, rather than the tenant farmers. Similarly, they were concentrated on a handful of farms that had been taken in hand by the Knight estate: Hoar Oak, Badgworthy, Duredown, Toms Hill, Larkbarrow, Pinkery and Winstitchin. These properties served the main herdings in the north and centre of Exmoor: Larkbarrow, The Chains, South Forest (Deer Park), Duredown and Pinkery. Occasionally, a shepherd would be present at Cornham or Honeymead, but those farms were usually reserved for local tenant farmers. In the 1890s, the Wheal Eliza cottage became a new home for the shepherds as the south Forest herding was moved from the Deer Park to a new location. It was this concentration of shepherds on a few estate holdings that drew the attention of outside observers to the 'great northern colony' on Exmoor.

Conclusion: The End Result

In 1882, the local Assistant Commissioner to the Parliamentary enquiry into agricultural depression tried to put a positive gloss on the situation. 'If the bright hopes which were once cherished as to this estate have not been altogether fulfilled' that was because in the 1840s 'too much attention was paid to the growth of Corn' despite the unsuitability of soil, climate and elevation. More recently efforts had shifted to 'replace the natural growth of rough grass, bilberries, etc. by good pasture' (UKPP C.3375 Royal Commission on Agriculture 1882: 33). Others were less sanguine. In public debates about land reform in the 1880s, Exmoor became a by-word for worthless property. Sir Stafford Northcote played devil's advocate with Henry George's ideas for land nationalisation at a public meeting in Devon during the 1885 General Election. If the land area of Britain was divided up among his inhabitants, Northcote observed that everyone would obtain about 2 acres (0.8 ha) each.

> I should very much like to have the two acres in the heart of London. I think it would pay very well, better than on Dartmoor or Exmoor either (laughter); but we cannot all have our two acres in the heart of London. And now let me suppose that some honest labourer were given two acres of his own out upon Exmoor, what is he going to do with it? (a Voice: 'Cultivate it,' and another Voice: 'Starve on it') (*London Evening Standard*, 29 May 1885).

Four years earlier, Earl Fortescue objected in the Lords to the Irish Land Bill, claiming that the confiscation of estates (such as his own) would diminish the capital available for investment and lead to repeated subdivision of tenants' holdings. Landlords could give better employment to labourers in digging field drains. However,

> He confessed his doubts as to the reclamation of land and the great benefits expected from it, as he had seen attempts made to reclaim land on Dartmoor, on Exmoor, and in Lewes, and on his own Irish estate, and knew by experience that the result never quite equalled the promise, whether the work was done by companies or individuals.

This earned Fortescue a private rebuke from Frederic Knight, who complained that 'I thought I was doing fairly well, and am aggrieved to find that my *best* neighbour has published a contrary opinion' (DHC 1262M/0/E/5/3 F. W. Knight to Earl Fortescue n. d.). Fortescue's statement also proved somewhat ironic. In 1886, he and his son bought the reversion of the Knight estate on Exmoor, for £193,000 (Orwin and Sellick 1970: 137). Reclamation may not have been worth doing, but the fruits of the Knights' efforts were still an attractive proposition.

By the 1880s, therefore, Exmoor occupied a different place within the rhetoric about agriculture—as a well-intentioned failure. This was particularly galling for Frederic Knight, because the Exmoor estate now finally returned regular profits, despite the agricultural depression. When John Knight bought the Royal Forest of Exmoor, its rents were worth approximately 6*d.* per acre from summer grazing for approximately 25,000 sheep (TNA LR5/1/2 Account of William Lock, Lady Day 1814 to Lady Day 1817). By the time Frederic Knight died in 1897, even after the effects of the agricultural depression, the estate brought in approximately £6–7000 per annum (or approximately £3 per acre) (Orwin and Sellick 1970: 135; DHC 1262M/0/E/20/153 Exmoor Estate Rental Ladyday 1885). The difficulty was that, by 1886, accumulated mortgage debts totalled £123,060. Yet, although the Knights more or less broke even on their 70-year struggle with Exmoor, contemporaries lumped it together with the much more spectacular financial disasters of the Sutherland reclamation schemes, as steps too far on the road to agrarian improvement. Nineteenth-century Exmoor provides an object lesson in how imagined concepts such as 'internal colonialism' set the parameters for agrarian development, justifying action, defining 'success' or 'failure' and motivating activity on the ground for decades—in the face of daily confrontations with the unyielding, dispiriting, intractable reality.

References

Devon Heritage Centre

1262M/0/E/20/152 Knight Estate Accounts Crooked Post, 1857
1262M/0/E/20/152 Middle Long Holcombe 1864
1262M/0/E/20/152 Knight Estate Accounts Eastern Long Holcombe 1870
1262M/0/E/20/153 Eastern Long Holcombe 1875
1262M/0/E/20/153 Allotments at Great and Little Ashcombe 1876
1262M/0/E/20/153 Knight Estate Accounts Crooked Post 1877
1262M/0/E/20/153 Allotments at Ricksy Ball, 1873 and 1877.
1262M/0/E/20/153 Exmoor Estate Rental Ladyday 1885.
1262M/0/E/21/7 & 8 Robert Tait Little Sheep Diaries, 1876–1907 (transcript provided by 3394.HOC263 Friends of Hoar Oak Cottage Sheep Diary transcribing project 2014).
1262M/0/E/5/3 F. W. Knight to Earl Fortescue n.d.
1262M/0/E/5/3 Correspondence about Exmoor estate sale 1885–1886.
2579A/PR/1/15 Lynton Parish Marriage Register, William Davidson, 8 October 1870.

SOMERSET HERITAGE CENTRE

A/DVF/1/3 Accounts of James Hayes, 1879–1888
A/DVF/1/5 Accounts of George and William Hayes, 11 vols., 1862–1914
A/EJM/1/3/16 J. W. MacDonald to Frederic Knight, 17 June 1867.
A/EJM/1/3/16 William Scott to Frederick Smyth, 6 March 1867.
A/EJM/1/3/18 Frederick Smyth to Frederic Knight, 3 January 1868, 6 January 1868, 3 May 1868.
A/EJM/1/3/18 J. W. MacDonald to Frederic Knight, 20 June 1868.

SCOTLAND

The Patient Register of Kirkland's Asylum, Bothwell, Lanarkshire. https://www.scottishindexes.com/hentry.aspx?hid=648001

THE NATIONAL ARCHIVES (SCOTLAND) HTTPS://WWW.SCOTLANDSPEOPLE.GOV.UK/

1851 Census, 067/2/4, William Scott.
1871 Census, 772/1/2, Peter Murray; 634/1/10, John Gourdie; 607/6/7, James Johnstone; 772/1/2, Thomas Graham.

THE NATIONAL ARCHIVES (UK)

HO 107/936/10 1841 Census, Thomas Crick Sr.
HO 107/1890/361 1851 Census, Ellen Blake; 07/1891, John Rudd Sr.; 107/1892/387, William Crang Sr.
RG9/1607 1861 Census, John Tidball.
RG 10/2180/13 1871 Census, George Richards; 10/2358/5, William Hayes.
RG 11/2245/24 1881 Census, John Crang; 11/2358/80, Charity Hayes; 2242/126, George Brook.
Office of the Auditors of Land Revenue LR5/1/2 Account of William Lock, Deputy Forester, Concern Sheep and Colts Entered to Pasture on the Forest of Exmoor from Lady Day 1814 to Lady Day 1817.

UK PARLIAMENTARY PAPERS

Command Papers C.3375 Royal Commission on Agriculture: Reports of the Assistant Commissioners Southern District of England, Report by Mr Little on Devon, Cornwall, Dorset, and Somerset (1882), p. 33.
Command Papers C.7728 Royal Commission on Agriculture Report by Mr. R. Henry Rew (Assistant Commissioner) on North Devon (1895), Appendix C II, p. 54.

NEWSPAPERS

Bristol Mercury, 30 April 1870
Dorset County Chronicle, 14 December 1854.
Exeter and Plymouth Gazette, 15 June 1889, 10 March 1891, 14 August 1895
Express and Echo, 20 June 1879.
London Evening Standard, 29 May 1885
North Devon Journal, 15 January 1857, 13 January 1859, 15 September 1859; 21 March 1861, 14 May 1863, 20 April 1865, 6 December 1866, 21 October 1875, 4 November 1875, 6 Nov. 1876, 12 September 1877, 8 July 1880, 13 March 1884, 4 September 1884, 14 September 1893, 8 May 1895.
Western Times, 23 December 1854; 8 October 1867.
Pall Mall Gazette, 6 October 1883, 24 October 1883, 26 October 1883.
Taunton Courier and Western Advertiser, 2 February 1859, 30 March 1859, 8 June 1859, 11 April 1860, 31 July 1861, 2 April 1862, 2 September 1863, 3 October 1866, 30 October 1861, 13 July 1870, 6 September 1871.
The Leisure Hour, September 1885, A. W. Groser, 'Hunting the Wild Red Deer'.
West Somerset Free Press, 9 September 1876, 4 September 1880, 4 December 1880, 27 August 1881, 10 December 1881, 12 January 1884, 23 October 1886, 8 October 1892, 16 September 1893.
Western Daily Press, 3 November 1893.
Western Morning News, 23 July 1889.
Western Times, 7 November 1875, 15 February 1889, 1 October 1920

SECONDARY WORKS

Brassley, P. 2000. Livestock Breeds. In *The Agrarian History of England and Wales. Volume VII 1850–1914 Part One*, ed. E.J.T. Collins, vol. 2, 555–570. Cambridge: Cambridge University Press.
Burton, R.A. 1989. *The Heritage of Exmoor*. Maslands Ltd.
Collins, E.J.T. 2000. Food Supplies and Food Policy. In *The Agrarian History of England and Wales. Volume VII 1850–1914 Part One*, ed. E.J.T. Collins, vol. 2, 33–72. Cambridge: Cambridge University Press.
Dudley Stamp L. 1941. *Land of Britain Vol. 92 Devonshire*. London.
French, H. 2024. 'The Wild West of England': Enclosure, Stag-Hunting, and the Creation of New Popular Perceptions of Exmoor in the Nineteenth Century. *Cultural and Social History* 21 (4): 507–534. https://doi.org/10.1080/14780038.2024.2359502.
French, H., and L. Baker. 2023. 'The Result Never Quite Equalled the Promise': Risk, Reward, and Reclamation on Exmoor, 1840–1897. *Agricultural History Review* 71 (1): 45–65.

Friends of Hoar Oak Cottage. http://hoaroakcottage.org/2017/10/11/grahams/

Hegarty, C., and R. Wilson-North. 2014. *The Archaeology of Hill Farming on Exmoor*. Swindon: English Heritage.

Hide, N. 2013. Outline Family Tree of the Davidson Family Originally from Muirkirk Ayrshire, Later Shepherds on Exmoor. Clan Davidson Association. https://clandavidson.org.uk/resources/

Hoyle, R.W. 2016. Introduction. In *The Farmer in England, 1650–1980*, ed. R.W. Hoyle. Abingdon: Routledge.

Mills, D.R., and J. Mills. 1997. Farms, farmers and Farm Workers in the Nineteenth-Century Census Enumerators' Books: A Lincolnshire case-study. *Local Historian* 27 (3): 130–144. https://www.balh.org.uk/publication-tlh-the-local-historian-volume-27-number-3-august-1997.

Orr, W. 1982. *Deer Forests, Landlords and Crofters. The Western Highlands in Victorian and Edwardian Times*. Edinburgh: John Donald Publishers.

Orwin, C.S., and R.J. Sellick. 1970. *The reclamation of Exmoor Forest*. Newton Abbot: David & Charles.

Robinson, G.M. 1988. *Agricultural Change. Geographical Studies of British Agriculture*. Edinburgh: North British Publishing.

Simpson, D. 2022. Culmaily, a Model of Improvement: Reform, Resistance and Rationalisation in South-eastern Sutherland. In *Land Reform in the British and Irish Isles since 1800*, ed. S. Evans, T. McCarthy, and A. Tindley, 27–47. Edinburgh: Edinburgh University Press. https://doi.org/10.3366/edinburgh/9781474487689.003.0002.

The Four Cousins: John Renwick, William Johnstone, James Johnstone and William Davidson. http://www.peasantstopuddles.org/cousins.htm

Tindley, A. 2009. "The Iron Duke": Land Reclamation and Public Relations in Sutherland, 1868–95. *Historical Research* 82 (216): 303–319. https://doi.org/10.1111/j.1468-2281.2007.00441.x.

———. 2010. *The Sutherland Estate, 1850–1920: Aristocratic Decline, Estate Management and Land Reform*. Edinburgh: Edinburgh University Press. https://doi.org/10.1515/9780748642670.

Polemics and Practices

Abstract How far did the 'colonising' rhetoric improvement match the reality on Exmoor in this period? The chapter uses high-resolution palaeo-ecological sampling and analysis to chart the changes in the abundance of tree, shrub, sedge, grass and other herb species on five sites within the Knight estate—located in both 'improved' farmland and open moorland sites. The analysis also models the effects on these distributions of drainage, grazing density and burning (associated with moorland management and 'improvement' methods) over the last 500 years. By comparing these distributions before and after the enclosure of the Royal Forest, it illustrates the relatively limited amount of change after 1818. While the effects of widespread drainage were apparent in the samples, enclosure and agrarian failures before 1860 reduced the intensity of use in many areas compared to the Royal Forest, while improved grasslands remained small in extent despite attracting much publicity. Consequently, the nineteenth century was not a period of wholesale change in the palaeoecological record.

Keywords Interdisciplinary • Moorlands • Peatlands • Palaeoecology • Development • Reclamation • Landscape restoration • Nineteenth century • Methodology

It has become clear through the documentary work that the initial intensity of transformation of the Forest of Exmoor was considerable. Significant amounts of capital were invested in the bounding of the estate, draining of the moorlands and development of the built infrastructure, including establishing tenancies that further enclosed parts of the estate. It might be supposed that such investment would be reflected in major transformations of the landscape, and ecological systems. The strength of the rhetoric from those responsible for management of the estate is one of profound, and successful, transformation of the estate, as described in Chapters "Reassessing Reclamation Under John Knight, 1818–1842" and "Frederic Knight and Robert Smith, 1843–1862". The ecological interventions of the estate's management were repeatedly recast as a radical and transformative departure from their predecessors. The extent to which this rhetoric matches actual transformations of the ecological systems within the former Royal Forest remains untested. Nevertheless, the nineteenth century is seen by many to be the most important in the development of the historic environment and landscape character of the moor today (Orwin and Sellick 1970; Riley and Wilson-North 2001).

This rhetoric, and the degree to which the Knights fundamentally changed the upland, can be explored through examining evidence from a key element of the landscape that the family sought to change: the peat bogs that lay across the Forest of Exmoor. The bogs represent long-term archives of environmental changes across the upland. Peat bogs build up layer upon layer of material, through the undecomposed litter of the plants that grow upon their surface. High water tables create anaerobic conditions suitable for preservation of organic materials that otherwise would be lost. As these layers build up, they also trap environmental evidence from the wider landscape, notably pollen grains that are dispersed from the plants growing across the bogs, and the dry land around them, but also other material, including evidence of land management practices such as grazing and burning. By taking cores from the bogs, and carefully sampling from different depths of each core, a picture can be built up of changes in the mires and surrounding landscape via the pollen record. There is a tradition of pollen analytical research on Exmoor reaching back to the early 1970s, when the first detailed work was undertaken from cores on the blanket mires of The Chains (Merryfield and Moore 1974; Merryfield 1977). Subsequent work focused on the prehistoric and mediaeval field systems at Hoar and Codsend Moors in the late 1980s (Francis and Slater 1990, 1992). A campaign to place Exmoor in a wider context of landscape changes in the early mediaeval period saw renewed interest in pollen analysis in the early 2000s (Fyfe et al. 2003, 2004; Rippon et al. 2006), and subsequent projects focused on various different aspects of the palaeoecological record on Exmoor (e.g. Fyfe 2012), several of which were undertaken as part of work undertaken to mitigate historical drainage within programmes of peatland restoration (Davies 2012; Ombashi 2020).

THE NATURE OF THE LANDSCAPE IN 1816

When John Knight acquired Exmoor Forest, he took possession of an estate which was almost entirely devoid of woodland. The *Devizes and Wiltshire Gazette* states that, in 1835, 'excepting a few willows and thorns by the sides of rivulets, not a tree or bush out of Simonsbath estate is to be seen on the whole forest' (*Devizes and Wiltshire Gazette*, 18 June 1835). A survey report from 1651 described the Forest as 'very good sheep pasture, much of it overgrown by heather' (Siraut 2009). These descriptions are borne out by the previous pollen analytical work on Exmoor (Figs. 1 and 2). Deforestation of the native tree cover on the higher parts of Exmoor was largely accomplished by the end of the prehistoric period, with major transformations associated with the establishment of the first field systems in the middle Bronze Age (Fyfe 2012; Ombashi 2020; Ombashi and Løvschal 2023). Further deforestation occurred in the late Iron Age (Fyfe et al. 2003), likely relating to increases in the importance of sheep within Iron Age society (Albarella 2007). These acts of deforestation in later prehistory are likely to have been an important factor in the establishment of blanket peat and acidic soils on Exmoor, changing the nature of the soils through compaction and reduced drainage (Merryfield and Moore 1974).

The valleys around the fringes of the upland are likely to have retained managed woodland at least into the early mediaeval period, used to produce charcoal for local iron production (Fyfe et al. 2013), or for a wider variety of uses (Cannell 2005). The previous pollen work confirms the Forest as a largely treeless tract of open grass or heather heath in recent centuries, a description that would have applied equally to any point in time across the preceding two millennia. The landscape was not, though, homogenous. Differences across the open landscape can be seen in both space, and time, over the last two millennia, notably in cover of heather, sedges or grassland (Fyfe et al. 2018). These differences are likely related to aspects of land management, and the natural drainage. However, the landscape within the Royal Forest is not distinctive from that outside the boundary of the Forest, at least at resolutions employed by previous studies (Figs. 1 and 2).

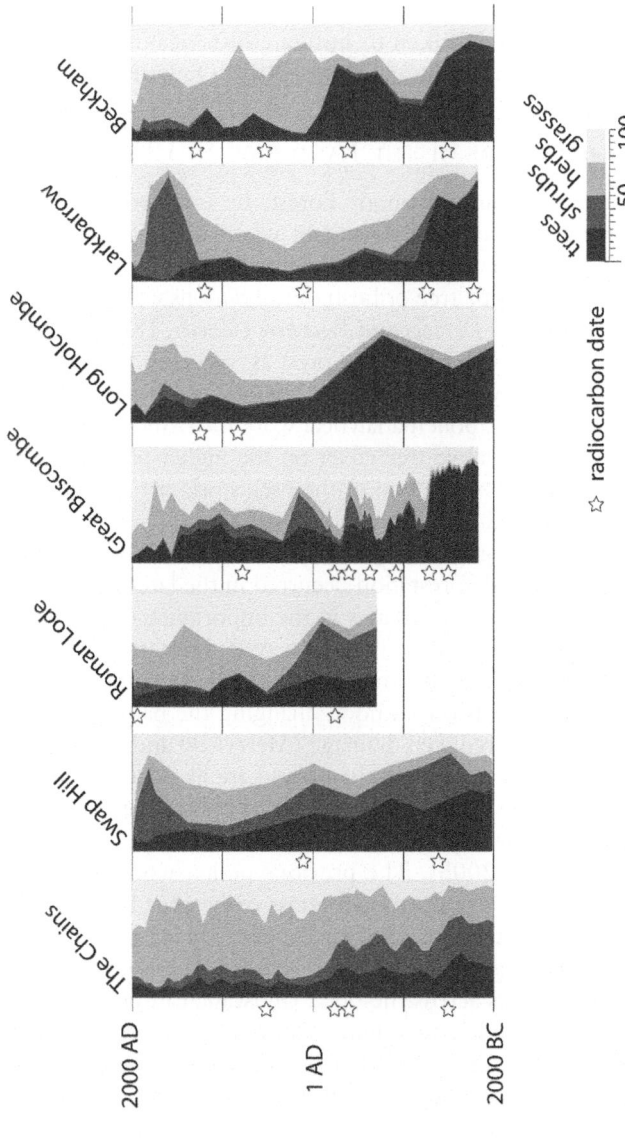

Fig. 1 Summary of low-resolution pollen sequences over the last 4000 years within the former Royal Forest of Exmoor. Stars indicate approximate positions of dates on each sequence

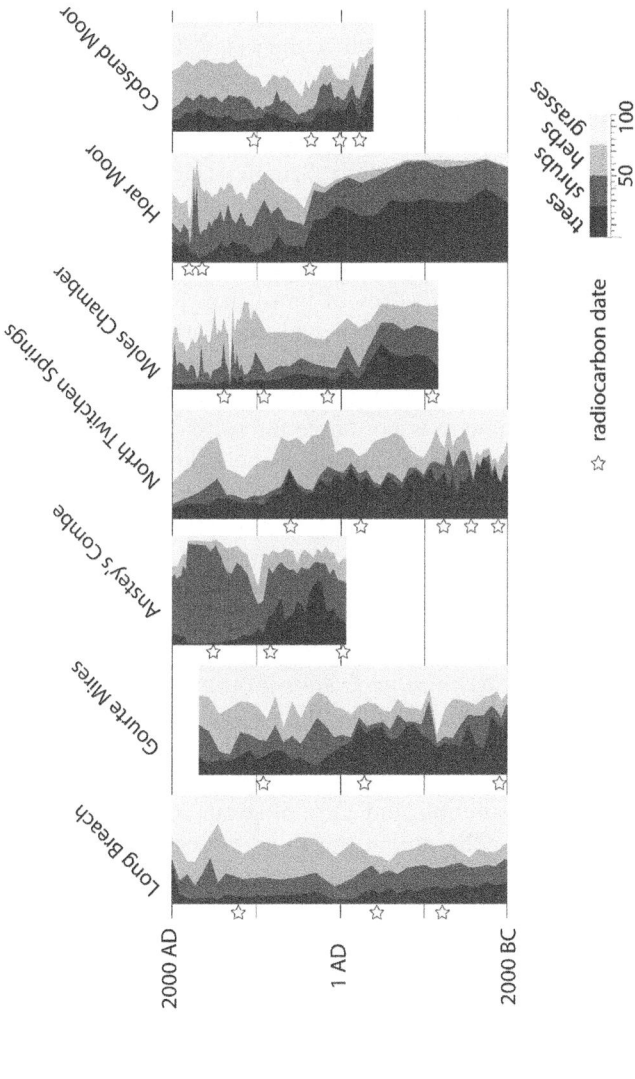

Fig. 2   Summary of low-resolution pollen sequences over the last 4000 years to 2020 from the wider Exmoor landscape, beyond the boundaries of the Royal Forest

THE NEW PALAEOECOLOGICAL WORK IN THE PROJECT

Whilst existing studies provide an overview of the development of the wider Exmoor landscape over the *longue durée*, it is challenging to use these data to understand the precise impact of the various waves of activity by the Knight family in the nineteenth century. This is a consequence of two factors. First, the published studies have largely focused on earlier periods of time (e.g. the prehistoric landscapes in Fyfe 2012, and Ombashi 2020, or the mediaeval landscape in Rippon et al. 2006) and recent periods generally have poor representation. Samples taken from peat cores were spaced out down the sequences to produce long-term records across the full depth of the peat. In most cases, this means a sample every 4 or 8 cm through cores typically 1–2 m long. This has resulted in low-resolution time-sequences, with gaps of more than 50 years, and more typically 100 years, between samples. Second, there are few chronological 'tie points' in these sequences to provide precise dating control (see Figs. 1 and 2). Generally, the upper levels of peat have been avoided as radiocarbon dating of recent sediments is a resource-intensive challenge, requiring many more dates to overcome deviations in the radiocarbon calibration curve caused by twentieth-century atomic weapons testing (the so-called 'bomb-carbon' effect: Goslar et al. 2005). Hence, prior to the 2010s, the sequences relating to recent centuries were poorly dated. This made it very difficult to comprehend properly the scale or intensity of landscape transformations brought about by the Knights via this long-term ecological record.

New work within the *Reclaiming Exmoor* project focused on five locations: Little Ashcombe, Ricksy Ball, The Chains, Larkbarrow, and Blackpitts (Fig. 3). These are distributed across the former Royal Forest, and the new work overcomes the challenges that exist in using the previous studies (temporal resolution, and chronological precision). Each location was managed differently during the Knights' tenure. Full details of the methodological approaches and results are published in Rowney et al. (2022, 2023). All but one of the sites are within the wider curtilage of farms established by the Knights. Little Ashcombe lies close to the early centrepiece of Simonsbath House Farm. The site has extensive deep drains and is also close to a series of hollow-ways leading up to what is the open moorland today, assumed to date from at least as early as the mediaeval period (Riley 2015). Ricksy Ball is within the enclosed land of Cornham Farm. Cornham was established by John Knight during the 1820s to

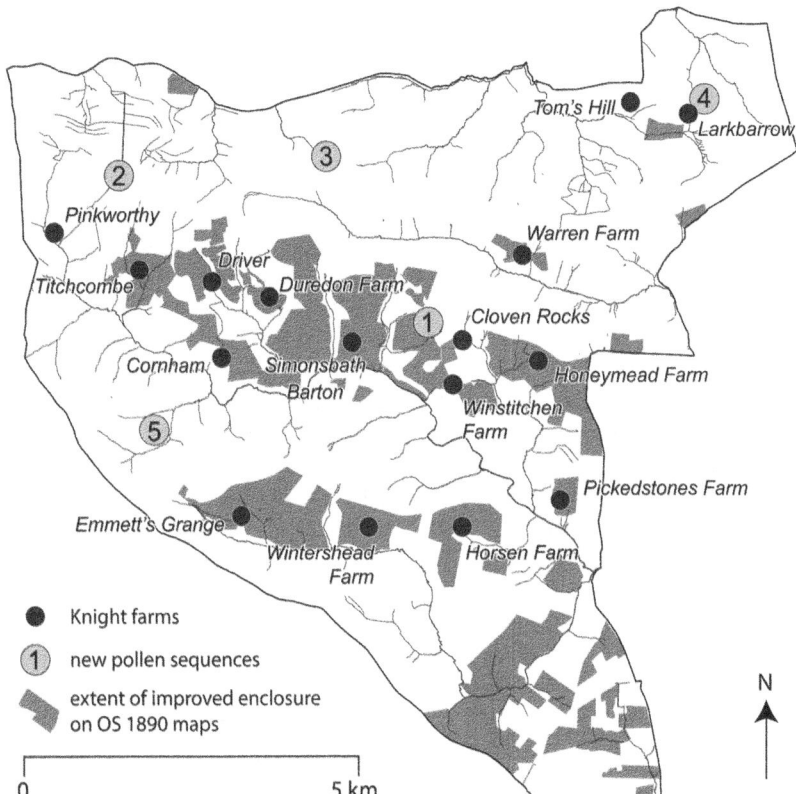

Fig. 3 Extent of improved enclosure at the end of the Knight period of ownership, based on the Ordnance Survey map transcription, location of Knight Farms, and pollen records in Rowney et al. (2022, 2023): (1) Little Ashcombe; (2) The Chains; (3) Blackpitts; (4) Larkbarrow; (5) Ricksy Ball

demonstrate agricultural improvement practices, and over 2 km of open drains across Ricksy Ball are recorded within the Knight archive. The Chains appears in the Knight archives as the most intensively drained peatland, with over 91 km of open drains cut, beginning immediately in 1819. The Chains was therefore clearly of importance, a central location for reclamation and drainage. Larkbarrow is one of the later farmsteads established under Frederic Knight's tenure. Drainage is relatively modest at

Larkbarrow (2 km of open drains are known to have been cut), undertaken in short bursts. At Larkbarrow, Smith implemented a system of herringbone 'catch meadow' drainage, to produce a radical transformation of the farm estate by establishing reliable hay cropping. Prior palaeoecological work at Larkbarrow (Davies et al. 2015) demonstrated survival of the peatland archive to the present day, in the mire in front of the farmstead site (see Fig. 4). Blackpitts lies at the eastern end of the central northern peatland belt, with The Chains at the western end. Blackpitts was largely preserved for turf cutting to provide fuel for firing local lime kilns (Riley 2014). The physical traces of this turf cutting are still evident, although the Blackpitts peatland complex has been part of the Exe Head peatland restoration programme since the late 1990s, and the deepest cuttings are in the process of regeneration behind significant dam complexes.

As the overarching aim of this part of the work was to evaluate changes in the ecology brought about by land management in the nineteenth century, the palaeoecological work covered both the last two centuries and extended across a longer period. In that way, detailed, decadal-scale records of at least the last 500 years at each site were developed to set any changes brought about by the Knights' tenure within the longer context. At each of the five locations, representative sequences of peat were extracted, either by coring, or where possible by opening small sections in the peat, providing larger volumes of material for study, sampled within monolith tins. Evidence for different land management practices was compiled directly from the peatland sequences, supplemented by documentary evidence from the Knight archive. Grazing intensity was estimated by identification and quantification of fungal spores associated with animal dung (*Sporormiella*, *Sordaria* and *Podospora* types). This method has been shown to produce reasonable estimates for grazing intensity from moorland contexts (Davies 2019), but it is not possible at present to equate fungal spore counts directly to animal numbers. Whilst herd sizes can be determined from the Knight archive and other historical sources (e.g. the Ministry of Agriculture returns from 1866 onwards), it is unclear how these animals were distributed across the estate, so differences in fungal spore concentrations both across time, and between locations, provide a useful proxy for understanding how grazing influenced the ecological conditions.

Fire has been an important upland land management tool for millennia (Fyfe et al. 2018), and the Knight archive reports peat burning (to improve soil fertility) and the common practice of burning heath to manipulate

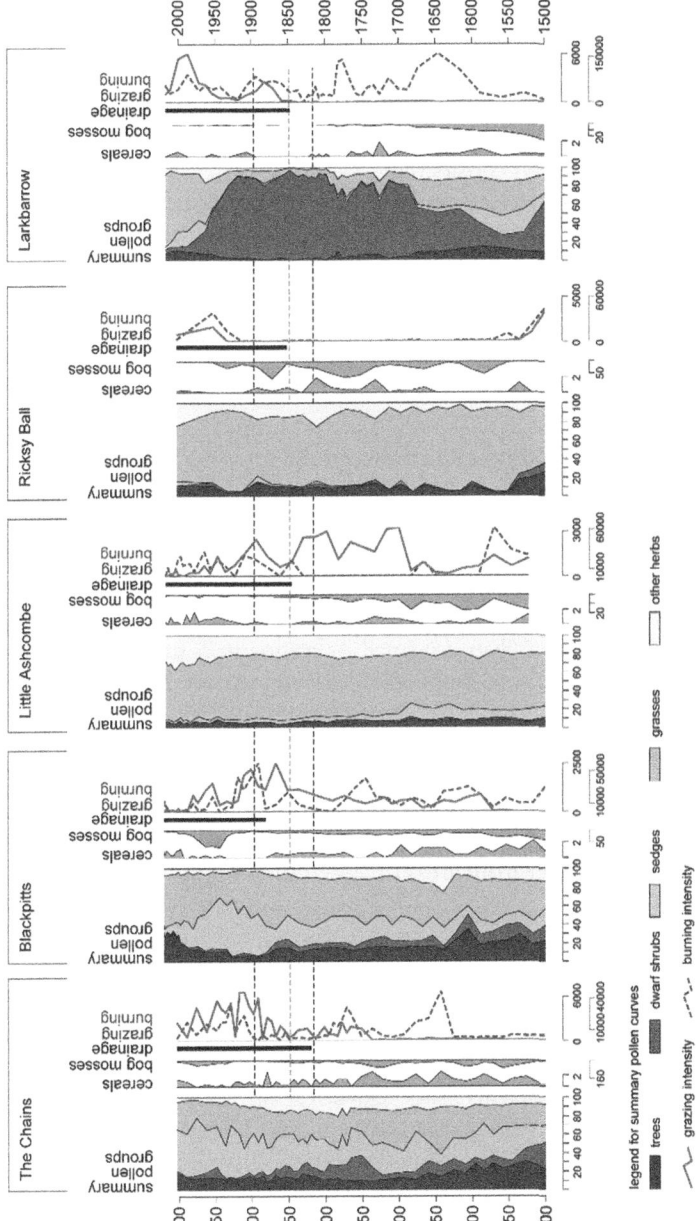

Fig. 4 Summary of pollen sequences in Rowney et al. (2022, 2023), and indications of land management practices (drainage, grazing, and burning)

vegetation structure. Evidence of burning around each of the five locations has been compiled by quantifying the abundance of microcharcoal deposition through time from each peatland record. Finally, the timing of drainage has been estimated for each site using the archival material. The intensity of drainage between sites, or the extent to which drains were maintained, has not been considered.

The impacts of these various land management practices have been evaluated by comparing them with highly resolved records of ecological change from the same cores. This has largely used pollen analysis, although, at some locations, change in the below-ground microbial communities has been explored. Exploratory work focused on testate amoebae, which are a crucial component of the microbial community of peatlands and are a top predator within the microbial food web (Davis and Wilkinson 2004). They are an important food source for chironomid (non-biting midge) larvae, and thus an important link between the microbial and invertebrate food chains, connecting to wider food webs, and thus a potentially valuable indicator of ecological health (Payne 2013). The pollen deposited on the peatland surface represents vegetation from both local plants (those growing directly on the peat itself), from the extra-local landscape (immediately around the peatland) and the wider region (perhaps as far as 10 km). The sites themselves are small in comparison to other locations used for pollen analysis (e.g. large lakes, or extensive wetlands), and most of the pollen was expected to come from the extra-local landscape (Jacobson and Bradshaw 1981). This is one of the main advantages of this sort of work on Exmoor: the palaeoecological record is firmly embedded within the historic landscape and can thus provide meaningful accounts of relatively local changes that are not possible from larger peat complexes that are typically further from areas of agricultural improvements.

DESCRIPTIONS OF THE KEY RESULTS

The new work has focused on recent centuries, and achieving the highest temporal resolution possible meant contiguous sampling of the upper levels of peat at either 0.5-cm or 1-cm intervals, informed either through existing outline work at each site (Davies et al. 2015 for Larkbarrow; Ombashi 2020 for The Chains) or 'rangefinder' dating. Rangefinder dating uses an initial set of radiocarbon dates (typically positioned at the top, middle and bottom of a core) to establish an outline chronological model. These outline chronologies were refined and finalised using additional suites of radiocarbon dates, combined with evidence of historical volcanic eruptions (mostly sourced from known Icelandic eruptions, with distinctive layers identified and characterised) and fallout radionucleides (Cs-137, Pb-210). Fallout radionucleides are particularly useful for establishing the dates of sediments in the last few hundred years. Peak counts of the Cs-137 radionucleide are associated with the Chernobyl disaster in 1986. The measurable amount of Pb-210 can provide precise dating of the last 200 years, as this naturally occurring isotope has a relatively short half-life (of 22.3 years). By combining these multiple lines of dating evidence using Bayesian approaches, it is possible to date individual samples with a high degree of certainty. This detailed programme of sampling and dating resulted in data points every 7–20 years across the last four centuries (Table 1).

A summary of the key analytical results is shown in Image 1. Image 1 also includes summaries of the main management approaches that have been inferred: dung fungi for grazing intensity; microcharcoal for burning; and the period during which drainage was undertaken. Focusing first

Table 1 Numbers of samples from each location from which pollen, dung fungal spores, and charcoal deposition have been assessed, and the time resolution that was achieved in the records

Site location	Number of pollen samples in last 1000 years	Number of dates	Age range (AD)	Sampling resolution (in years) between 1500 and 2000 AD
The Chains	61	10 radiocarbon,Cs-137, Pb-210	1405–2005	7
Blackpitts	50	13 radiocarbon,Cs-137, Pb-210,3 tephra horizons	1440–2020	10
Little Ashcombe	39	6 radiocarbon,Cs-137, Pb-210,2 tephra horizons	1520–2015	12
Ricksy Ball	34	8 radiocarbon,Cs-137, Pb-210,2 tephra horizons	1030–2005	20
Larkbarrow	48	5 radiocarbon,Cs-137, Pb-210,1 tephra horizon	1400–2020	9

Image 1   Dr Fran Rowney sampling peat at Larkbarrow 2022. (Note: The sampling site is adjacent to the Knight farmstead, marked by the beech trees planted to provide shelter in the exposed location)

on the summary pollen data, when John Knight made his purchase, The Chains and Blackpitts were healthy blanket mires, characterised by a mix of heather, grasses and sedges, in a largely treeless landscape. Whilst there is slightly more woodland represented in these two blanket mire sites in comparison to the other three sites, the higher position of these bogs in the landscape meant that they are likely to have captured tree pollen from managed woodland in the lower valleys around the upland (Cannell 2005). The landscapes around Little Ashcombe and Ricksy Ball were almost entirely dominated already by grassland, with Little Ashcombe having a little more sedge. Both Little Ashcombe and Ricksy Ball also have a higher proportion of 'other herbaceous' types. Rowney et al. (2022, 2023) show that these low-growing plants are typically plantains, sorrels, buttercups and cinquefoils. These taxa are typical indicators of grazed grassland (Mazier et al. 2006; Gaillard and Fyfe 2024). Grasses, and grassland-associated species, make up most of the pollen types identified at Little Ashcombe and Ricksy Ball. 'Other herbaceous' plants are typically under-represented in the pollen record, as they tend to be insect polli-nated, or release their pollen close to the ground, resulting in limited dis-persal in comparison to taller, wind-pollinated vegetation (Broström et al. 2008). It is therefore safe to assume that these locations were species-rich, wide-open grasslands at the start of the nineteenth century. Larkbarrow is conspicuously different to the other sites: the record is dominated by heathers and dwarf shrubs, which had been pre-eminent since the late seventeenth century. Prior to this, in the mid-sixteenth century, the land-scape around Larkbarrow had been a mixture of heath, species-rich grass-land, and mosses and sedges. These data confirm that John Knight purchased an estate that was overwhelmingly open and support contem-porary accounts of a treeless upland with rich pasture, but one that was variable in character. There were sedge and moss-rich areas of bog (such as The Chains), good pasture, and extensive tracts of heather.

It is unclear why Larkbarrow became a heather-dominated area from the mid-sixteenth century. Modern ecological observations associate heather dominance with burning regimes, and grazing tends to reduce heathers, as these plants are less tolerant of trampling and nibbling, and promote grasses instead (Pakeman and Nolan 2009). At Larkbarrow, though, the initial rise of heather is coincident with evidence of a period of grazing starting in the late sixteenth century, lasting for perhaps 60–70 years, but with little evidence of fire to control vegetation. Hobbs and Gimingham (1987) have shown that light to moderate grazing may sus-tain heathland. This suggests that although grazing in the Forest was known to have occurred in the seventeenth century (and see discussion below for a comparison of grazing intensity across time), it was not suffi-ciently intensive at Larkbarrow to produce widespread grassland. In fact, it was only once the intensity of grazing declined that heather became hyper-dominant at Larkbarrow (Image 1).

Consequences of John Knight's Purchase of the Estate

There is little in the pollen data to mark the purchase of the Royal Forest by John Knight. The first half of the nineteenth century is best character-ised as a period of continuity in land cover, rather than abrupt change. Detailed analysis by Rowney et al. (2023) using 'rate of change' analysis has shown that, far from being a period of profound changes to the veg-etation, the upland largely remained the same, at least from the perspec-tive offered by pollen analysis. Why might this be, particularly when so much is made of the transformative effect of the Knights' tenure? There is no doubt that the physical infrastructure of enclosure, construction of farming facilities and extensive drainage may have given the visual impres-sion of great and energetic change, and these undertakings no doubt con-sumed capital, expended on materials and labour. The significance of livestock, and in particular stocking densities, may well be the key. Livestock occupied a central role in how nineteenth-century writers envi-sioned the 'success' or 'failure' of ecological interventions. The combined emotional and economic connection to 'living capital' imbued animals with immense importance (Griffin 2012). John Knight eliminated the customary practice of communal sheep grazing on Exmoor in 1819. In place of native traditions of sheep management, he imported breeds of Scotch Cattle deemed fashionable at the time. Despite his previously noted investments in drainage, irrigation and liming, this 'improved' herd only ever reached 1197 heads (Baker et al. 2024). The near absence of evidence for grazing is notable in the palaeoecological sequences: there are few fungal spores recorded at any of the five sites, suggesting very low levels of grazing at most, and at The Chains, Blackpitts and Larkbarrow, grazing intensity was lower than that seen in the preceding centuries. There is also limited evidence for changes in burning regimes. The datas-ets shown in Image 1 show that fire was already part of the management systems on Exmoor but perhaps only came into consciousness within the nineteenth-century archival material.

Whilst the overall character of the upland vegetation may not have changed, the imposition of drainage, particularly across The Chains and Little Ashcombe, is associated with reductions in bog mosses and should have influenced these deeper peatland systems. Rowney et al. (2023) have shown that drainage had a significant effect on the abundance of *Sphagnum* moss. These bryophytes are particularly sensitive to reductions in the water table associated with drainage, and the change may have shifted the bog communities away from sedge- and moss-rich communities towards grasses, particularly purple moorgrass (*Molinia caerulea*; see discussion in Chambers et al. 1999). Drainage may also have had significant effects on the ecology of the below-ground microbial communities, an aspect of the environment that would have been unfamiliar to the nineteenth-century agrarian observer and remains reasonably obscure today. In the detailed study of Ricksy Ball, Rowney et al. (2022) demonstrated that although vegetation exhibited only modest change (the loss of *Sphagnum*), and insect assemblages showed little change, the microbial communities (as reflected in assemblages of the single-celled testate amoebae) were rapidly transformed and are yet to recover. The implications of these below-ground changes remain unclear but may have affected the foundational food webs across the bogs. Below-ground food webs are connected to above-ground communities, as they provide the foundational level for the insects that support moorland birds: changes in one part of the system are likely to cascade to other trophic levels (Sasaki et al. 2022).

EFFECTS OF THE CREATION OF FARMS AND THE SMITH/ SMYTH REGIMES

In the 1840s, Frederic Knight completed the initial infrastructure around the main tenant farms, and the enclosure of large fields around them. The early tenancies had enclosed almost 5000 acres (2023 ha), at Emmett's Grange (1300 acres/526 ha), Cornham (545 acres/221 ha), Honeymead (2100 acres/850 ha) and Simonsbath Barton (1030 acres/417 ha). Frederic Knight completed the enclosure of a further 2600 acres (1052 ha) (Driver: 400 acres/162 ha, Duredon 900 acres/364 ha, Warren 700 acres/283 ha), Horsen 400 acres/162 ha, Wintershead 200 acres/81 ha). A further 1557 acres (630 ha) were designated at

Pinkery (400 acres/162 ha), Titchcombe (557 acres/225 ha) and Cornham Hill (600 acres/243 ha) but are not recorded as completed by the end of the 1840s. Thus, by the late 1840s, around four-tenths of the 20,000-acre estate had been enclosed for over a decade, with more designated.

On the surface, the transformation of so much of the estate by the end of the 1840s should have had a far more obvious transformative impact on the ecological systems. Farmsteads and outbuildings were constructed to varying levels of completeness. Guidance for fencing was established, with construction the responsibility of the tenants and their own capital (with rental reductions in compensation). However, significant and long-term changes from the late 1840s are hard to discern in the vegetation records. Both Ricksy Ball and Little Ashcombe continue to show a completely open, grassland-dominated landscape. Whilst there is some marginal change in heather cover at Larkbarrow, there is no major transformation to grass dominance. Why was continuity the norm? In part, this must relate to the intensity of activity. There was never a period when all, or even the majority, of the tenancies were in active management. According to Orwin (1929), Larkbarrow, Tom's Hill, Duredon, Winstitchen, Pinkery, Titchcombe, and Wintershead were vacant in the late 1860s, a total of more than 3000 acres (1214 ha), and more than 8000 acres (3237 ha) of the estate had never been enclosed. The desire amongst the estate's management to 'conquer the rugged moor' at any cost, combined with overly optimistic expectations of Exmoor's potential, and the neglect of infrastructure, created an impossible situation for the largely inexperienced and unsupported tenants. Due to the frantic pace of farm building between 1844 and 1852, many tenants arrived to find their holdings incomplete and unsuitable for habitation and agriculture. Throughout the next decade, financial failure caused by the loss of vital stock and crops to inadequate shelter, fencing, drainage and infrastructure would become commonplace for many new tenants. William Hannam commented on the misfortunes of James Coombes at Crooked Post who bought 500 sheep in the autumn of 1845, when 'there was a great Scarcetey of Keep the winter they gott very Poor I have hird they were scarcely able to walk down in the Spring—He had onley 400 Acres of Land and not a Foot of it Cultivated or fit for that Class of Sheep—The Concequence was the whole of them gott in such a weak state they Died' (Orwin and Sellick 1970: 254). Similarly, James Meadows quickly ran into financial trouble, because he brought high-quality cattle to the complete unimproved pastures of Larkbarrow, where Hannam noted 'no Land or verey little that had bin nearely Seeded out and his Land in genaral was produsing verey indifferent pasture' (Orwin and Sellick 1970: 265). Soon the 'stock was going back in Condition instead of Forward', and Meadows was forced to sell them at a loss because he lacked the fodder to keep them through winter. Between 1844 and 1862, the first generation of Exmoor tenants endured unfinished farmsteads, barns and outbuildings, insufficient improved land for fodder or roots, and the absence of basic infrastructure, such as drains and fences. These problems deprived tenants of the chance to establish even a financial foothold on Exmoor and made long-term reclamation projects inconceivable.

These issues were compounded by other problems, such as the harsh winters. John Knight's purchase of the estate came towards the end of the Little Ice Age, a broad period between c. 1650 and c. 1900 characterised by average summer temperatures that were cooler than those in the late twentieth century (Matthews and Briffa 2005). Whilst summer temperatures were on average a little lower across the northern hemisphere, temperatures across Europe did not fall to the same extent. Increases in winter precipitation may have been more significant, which on Exmoor produced repeated heavy snowfalls. It has been argued that the Little Ice Age posed challenges to pastoralism in upland regions, particularly by reducing the availability of winter fodder (Costello et al. 2023). Analysis of the economic impact of the Little Ice Age in Europe has suggested a limited impact of weather on harvests (Kelly and Ó Gráda 2020); however, the analysis of climate data within Kelly and Ó Gráda (2020) showed that winter weather conditions showed greater year-on-year variability than had previously been assumed. The consequences of unpredictable, and variable, amounts of heavy snowfall compounded the difficulties for the tenants of the Knight farms, particularly without the infrastructure required to shelter their animals. Men from the east of England, who may have had experience with cold, but stable, winters, may not have had a sufficient understanding of the unpredictable, and frequently varied, weather conditions of southwest Britain.

Undoubtedly, land improvement methods on some of the estate farms were advanced and transformative. Smith's work at Emmett's Grange is well documented in the Knight archive, and immediately on taking over the holding, he began improving the surrounding landscape 'breaking ground and carrying lime fast, and cutting into the long spring and thoroughly draining every bog as he comes to it' (SHC A/EJM/1/1/6

Frederic Knight to John Knight, 21 August 1848). The farms of the south Forest that lay close to Emmett's Grange saw sustained level of improvement (Fig. 3) and were the more popular tenancies. These farms were the 'pet projects' of Smith as the largely untouched lands here allowed him to 'make his mark' and ensure that the farms ran exactly to his vision of how an upland farm 'should be'. The farms of the 'central belt', in the areas worked by John Knight, received only a moderate level of improvement and had tenants with serious financial difficulties, perhaps limiting their ability to make substantive improvements to the land. The northern Forest farms, including Larkbarrow and Tom's Hill, saw little improvement (Image 1) and were left to deteriorate: by the 1890s, there is little evidence of improved moorland in contemporary mapping. The failure to secure a reliable and cost-effective source of lime for soil improvement also thwarted the ambition for wholescale change. It is perhaps therefore not surprising that ecological systems show few changes, when most of the estate was not in active management and was largely unable to effect wholescale change in soil pH through the addition of lime. It must also be remembered that the Royal Forest was not a *tabula rasa*, an untouched and untamed wilderness, despite contemporary depictions in the popular press (French 2024). The landscape had already been transformed by dozens of generations of farmers who used the Forest for grazing prior to the sale of the estate. Soils had also been impacted by legal turbary from within the forest: MacDermot (1973, 215) cites reports of a commercial turf cutter in Bray who could cut 1600 turves a day in 1635.

Both contemporary commentators and twentieth-century historians have perceived the return of sheep as monumental moment in the ecological evolution of Exmoor. Smith, and then Smyth, oversaw the reintroduction of sheep ranching onto the estate. The Knight family's sheep herds, which were virtually non-existent in 1862, grew to 15,877 animals in 1897 (3394.HOC263 Diaries of Robert Tait Little). Evidence for these animals can be seen within increasing numbers of dung fungal spores at Little Ashcombe and Larkbarrow (Image 1), and at Larkbarrow, grazing may have been responsible for a reduction in the abundance of heather, replaced by grass, although only briefly: the major shift to grassland around Larkbarrow does not come about until the early twentieth century.

The visible presence of sheep on the moorland led contemporary agriculturalists to declare that the estate had become 'extremely good land for stocking' and promoted a narrative of the Knight family's success, based on transforming a landscape of 'unsound pastures' to 'healthy feeding grounds' hosting a 'higher order of grasses and clovers'. Stocking densities on the Knight estate are, though, lower than those in the surrounding parishes (Baker et al. 2024; Darby 1873), and the number of animals on the upland by 1897 was far from unprecedented. By the sixteenth century, the Crown was leasing the Forest to those who could make money by charging for grazing, and the number of sheep was estimated at 43,000. The number of sheep declined significantly when payment to graze animals rose in the 1630s, to around 16,000 animals—surprisingly like the number at the end of Frederic Knight's tenure (Siraut 2009). In 1813, the enclosure commissioners estimated that in the previous century 32,000 sheep would have been admitted onto Exmoor 'in a usual year' (NA CRES/2/1503 Survey and Report of the Forest of Exmoor by Richard Hawkins). These high stocking densities before the advent of the Knights' tenure created the open, grass-dominated, character of the upland, most likely extending back into the mediaeval period (Albarella 2007). Ironically, therefore, since it took most of the nineteenth century to return sheep numbers to their historic levels, the advent of sheep herdings did not have a transformative ecological effect, beyond maintaining the *status quo* of open grassland.

SOME CAVEATS ABOUT THE USE OF POLLEN RECORDS

Pollen provides an excellent source of information that can describe aspects of the ecological system in detail that can be both spatially and temporally precise. However, there are limitations. The beech trees that were used for hedging and fencing from the 1850s are notable for their near absence in most of the pollen records, both new and existing. The Knight archive indicates the importance that Smith placed on trees for protection of the new farms from the ravages of the Exmoor weather, from the early 1850s onwards. Smith requested 3630 trees and saplings to be planted around parts of the North Forest. Hence, beech trees were planted in their thousands, with nurseries established in the 1850s to sustain the requirement for plants, for example, a new plantation of beech and Scots pine in 1854 at Halscombe Hill. The invisibility of beech in the pollen records is explicable by understanding the reproductive cycle of beech trees. Beech trees generally do not begin flowering until they reach 40 years of age when they are grown in the open, and not until 60–80 years when they are in dense stands (Packham et al. 1992). Repeated cutting to produce dense hedges is likely to have prevented trees from flowering. It is probable, therefore, that beech pollen would only become evident at the end of the nineteenth century, provided that those trees were not regularly pollarded, or managed for hedging.

Two further observations about the pollen record are also worthy of consideration: the scale of landscape which is represented by the sequences, and the ability to differentiate within broad groups of plants. Individual pollen records do not provide a holistic view of ecological change across an entire landscape, that is, the entirety of the 22,000-acre (8903 ha) estate. As discussed at the beginning of this chapter, they will capture most of their pollen from the extra-local area around each site. Defining the precise size of the 'extra-local' area is challenging, although Rowney et al. (2023) suggested that most pollen might come from within 1 km of the coring site based on theoretical considerations and empirical data (Sugita 1994; Fyfe et al. 2003; Bunting and Hjelle 2010). This equates to an area of perhaps 800 acres (324 ha). Placing these areas on the map (Fig. 3), alongside the areas covered by the prior (albeit less well-resolved temporal) sequences (e.g. see Fyfe et al. 2018), achieves good coverage of the northern Forest, the centre of the estate around Simonsbath, and some of the southern Forest. Gaps in coverage remain, though, including around Emmett's Grange, the central belt (e.g. Honeymead Farm) and some eastern tenant farms (such as Horsen and Pickedstones).

The second consideration is the degree to which pollen grains can be attributed to individual plant species. There are frustrations, particularly for the family of grasses, which cannot be distinguished based on their morphology: all grass species (with the exception of cereals) look the same. We know that the Knights introduced new species of grass, but at present, these cannot be differentiated from the native species. New chemical techniques that can separate the pollen grains of different species of moorland grasses are promising for future research (e.g. Scoble et al. 2024), but these methods are not yet sufficiently advanced for application to sub-fossil material. It is possible to look more broadly at the communities of plants that are associated with grassland, that is, the other species associated with unimproved moorland, and consider how the broad grassland communities change. There are no obvious patterns, although over time there is a general reduction of some of the key grassland-associated types (in particular, the plantains decline across the late nineteenth and early twentieth centuries). At most sites, this decline in plantains reflects a general reduction in the diversity of the open-ground pollen types. The implication is that the moorland may have become increasingly species-poor, perhaps through sowing new varieties or by the increasing dominance of purple moor grass (Chambers et al. 1999). Rowney et al. (2023) have shown that reduced pollen richness is associated with both intensity of grazing and drainage.

The palaeoecological findings are that landscape transformation was far more limited than existing studies suggest. Rising sheep and cattle numbers through the later nineteenth century need to be considered against the large area of land available on Exmoor: the 'grand experiments' conducted by Smyth had little long-term impact on stocking rates (Sidney 1878). Crop acreages data (see Fig. 5 in Baker et al. 2024) showed momentary spikes in rape and wheat at the beginning of Smyth's 'reclamation' project, but the acreage devoted to these plants quickly declined, and these practices have not been identified within the pollen record. Pollen from the Brassica family (evidence of rape cultivation) is found sporadically throughout the sequences at Larkbarrow and Ricksy Ball, but from the seventeenth century onwards, and is not restricted to the nineteenth century. Pollen from cereals follows a similar pattern: all sequences have sporadic low counts for cereals pollen types across the last 500 years, and although pollen from cereals is notoriously under-represented in the pollen record (Behre 1986; Gaillard and Fyfe 2024), the sequences probably pick up a wider agrarian signal from the surrounding parishes. Land use on Exmoor during the Knights' tenure, from a palaeoecological perspective, was not particularly unique or innovative. During the latter half of the nineteenth century, Exmoor was (re-)incorporated into the agricultural and environmental trends of the North Devon and West Somerset region. There is the suggestion of a return to traditional methods as an increasing number of formerly excluded 'local' farmers began to take land in the form of allotments and individual fields, and these are visible as improved land on the maps of the 1890s (e.g. the small pieces of improved enclosure in the south and east of the estate: Fig. 3). As has been outlined, grazing on the Knight estate was probably less intensive than the common grazing regime on Exmoor throughout the seventeenth and eighteenth centuries (MacDermot 1973). Far from being a moment of 'revolution', the purchase of the estate by John Knight resulted in stocking rates plummeting. Reduction in stock might have had consequences for ecological 'recovery', for example, growth of woody shrubs (expansion of heather) or a shift to rougher moorland vegetation, as was observed with the abandonment of some mediaeval settlements on other southwest uplands (Austin and

Walker 1985). John and Frederic Knight's improvements may have mitigated such recovery despite reduced stocking numbers. Drainage would
have created drier conditions, and burning would have controlled heather.
Taking both the documentary and palaeoecological evidence together,
though, there is little evidence that the Knights enacted any major ecological changes. In the last decade, a great deal of energy and resources has
been devoted to making reparations to the shallow peatland areas that
were the focus of so much drainage by the Knight family (Grand-Clement
et al. 2013). Five years of monitoring work observing the impacts of
blocking drainage ditches has not been able to show any significant
changes in the dominant (grass-dominated) vegetation or any major and
sustained changes in the water tables in the areas characterised by thin
peaty soils (Gatis et al. 2020). The suggestion by Gatis is that modern
management needs to be bolder (a greater level of intervention), or that
vegetation may take much longer to adjust to restoration practices. An
alternative perspective, informed by a new understanding of the limited
overall impact of Knights' efforts, might conclude that drainage in the
mid-nineteenth century of what are described as 'shallow, marginal peatlands' was never as transformative as the family hoped, and contemporary
commentators believed. This does not preclude the fact that changes
could be locally very significant, particularly by extensive cutting in the
deeper peats, for example, at Blackpitts, but these effects were most probably localised, rather than systemic across the whole landscape.

References

SOMERSET HERITAGE CENTRE

A/EJM/1/1/6 Frederic Knight to John Knight, 21 August 1848

THE NATIONAL ARCHIVES (UK)

CRES/2/1503 A Survey and Report of the Forest of Exmoor in the Counties of
    Somerset and Devon by Richard Hawkins of Kingsbridge in 1812 & 1813.

NEWSPAPERS

Devizes and Wiltshire Gazette, 18 June 1835

PRIMARY PRINTED SOURCES

Darby, J. 1873. The Farming of Somerset. *Journal of the Bath and West of England Society* 5: 105–106.

SECONDARY WORKS

Albarella, U. 2007. The End of the Sheep Age: People and Animals in the Late Iron Age. In *The later Iron Age in Britain and beyond*, ed. C. Haselgrove and T. Moore. Oxford and Oakville CT: Oxbow Books.

Austin, D., and M.C. Walker. 1985. A New Landscape Context for Houndtor, Devon. *Medieval Archaeology* 29: 147–152. https://doi.org/10.5284/1071716.

Baker, L., F. Rowney, H. French, and R. Fyfe. 2024. Revolution and Continuity? Reassessing Nineteenth-Century Moorland Reclamation Through Palaeoecological and Historical Research. *Landscape Research* 49: 48–63. https://doi.org/10.1080/01426397.2023.2244904.

Behre, K.E. 1986. *Anthropogenic Indicators in Pollen Diagrams*. AA Balkema.

Broström, A., A.B. Nielsen, M.J. Gaillard, K. Hjelle, F. Mazier, H. Binney, M.J. Bunting, R.M. Fyfe, V. Meltsov, A. Poska, S. Räsänen, W. Soepboer, H. Stedingk, H. Suutari, and S. Sugita. 2008. Pollen Productivity Estimates of Key European Plant Taxa for Quantitative Reconstruction of Past Vegetation: a Review. *Vegetation History and Archaeobotany* 17: 461–478. https://doi.org/10.1007/s00334-008-0148-8.

Bunting, M.J., and K.L. Hjelle. 2010. Effect of Vegetation Data Collection Strategies on Estimates of Relevant Source Area of Pollen (RSAP) and Relative Pollen Productivity Estimates (relative PPE) for Non-arboreal Taxa. *Vegetation History and Archaeobotany* 19: 365–374. https://doi.org/10.1007/s00334-010-0246-2.

Cannell, J.A. 2005. *The Archaeology of Woodland Exploitation in the Greater Exmoor Area in the Historic Period*. BAR Publishing.

Chambers, F.M., D. Mauquoy, and P.A. Todd. 1999. Recent Rise to Dominance of Molinia Caerulea in Environmentally Sensitive Areas: New Perspectives from Palaeoecological Data. *Journal of Applied Ecology* 36: 719–733. https://doi.org/10.1046/j.1365-2664.1999.00435.x.

Costello, E., K. Kearney, and B. Gearey. 2023. Adapting to the Little Ice Age in Pastoral Regions: An Interdisciplinary Approach to Climate History in North-West Europe. *Historical Methods: a journal of Quantitative and Interdisciplinary History* 56: 77–96. https://doi.org/10.1080/01615440.2022.2156958.

Davies, H. 2012. Sustainable Management of the Historic Environment Resource in upland Peat. Unpublished PhD thesis, University of Plymouth. https://pearl.plymouth.ac.uk/cgi/viewcontent.cgi?article=1520&context=gees-theses

Davies, H., R.M. Fyfe, and D. Charman. 2015. Does Peatland Drainage Damage the Palaeoecological Record? *Review of Palaeobotany and Palynology* 221: 92–105. https://doi.org/10.1016/j.revpalbo.2015.05.009.

Davis, S.R., and D.M. Wilkinson. 2004. The Conservation Management Value of Testate Amoebae as 'Restoration' Indicators: Speculations Based on Two Damaged Raised Mires in Northwest England. *Holocene* 14: 135–143. https://doi.org/10.1191/0959683604hl696rp.

Davies, A.L. 2019. Dung Fungi as an Indicator of Large Herbivore Dynamics in Peatlands. *Review of Palaeobotany and Palynology* 271: 104–108. https://doi.org/10.1016/j.revpalbo.2019.104108.

Francis, P.D., and D.S. Slater. 1990. A Record of Vegetation and Land Use Change from Upland Peat Deposits on Exmoor. Part 2: Hoar Moor. *Proceedings of the Somerset Archaeology and Natural History Society* 134: 1–25.

———. 1992. A Record of Vegetational and Land Use Change from Upland Peat Deposits on Exmoor. Part 3: Codsend Moors. *Proceedings of the Somerset Archaeological and Natural History Society* 136: 9–28.

French, H. 2024. 'The Wild West of England': Enclosure, Stag-Hunting, and the Creation of New Popular Perceptions of Exmoor in the Nineteenth Century. *Cultural and Social History* 21 (4): 507–534. https://doi.org/10.1080/14780038.2024.2359502.

Fyfe, R.M. 2012. Bronze Age Landscape Dynamics: Spatially Detailed Pollen Analysis from a Ceremonial Complex. *Journal of Archaeological Science* 39: 2764–2773. https://doi.org/10.1016/j.jas.2012.04.015.

Fyfe, R.M., A.G. Brown, and S.J. Rippon. 2003. Mid- to Late-Holocene Vegetation History of Greater Exmoor, UK: Estimating the Spatial Extent of Human-induced Vegetation Change. *Vegetation History and Archaeobotany* 12: 215–232. https://doi.org/10.1007/s00334-003-0018-3.

———. 2004. Characterising the Late Prehistoric, "Romano-British" and Medieval Landscape, and Dating the Emergence of a Regionally distinct Agricultural System in South West Britain. *Journal of Archaeological Science* 31: 1699–1714. https://doi.org/10.1016/j.jas.2004.05.003.

Fyfe, R.M., L. Bray, G. Juleff, J. Woodbridge, and P. Marshall. 2013. The Environmental Impact of Romano-British Ironworking on Exmoor. In *The World of Iron*, ed. J. Humphris and T. Rehren, 462–472. Archetype Publications.

Fyfe, R.M., H. Ombashi, H. Davies, and K. Head. 2018. Quantified Moorland Vegetation and Assessment of the Role of Burning Over the Past Five Millennia. *Journal of Vegetation Science* 29: 393–403. https://doi.org/10.1111/jvs.12594.

Gaillard, M.J., and R.M. Fyfe. 2024. Reconstructing Past Human Impact on Vegetation Using Pollen Data. In *Encyclopaedia of Quaternary Science*. Elsevier.

Gatis, N., D.J. Luscombe, P. Benaud, J. Ashe, E. Grand-Clement, K. Anderson, I.P. Hartley, and R.E. Brazier. 2020. Drain Blocking has Limited Short-term Effects on Greenhouse Gas Fluxes in a Molinia caerulea Dominated Shallow Peatland. *Ecological Engineering* 158: 1060–1079. https://doi.org/10.1016/j. ecoleng.2020.106079.

Goslar, T., W.O. van der Knaap, S. Hicks, M. Andrič, J. Czernik, E. Goslar, S. Räsänen, and H. Hyötylä. 2005. Radiocarbon Dating of Modern Peat Profiles: Pre-and Post-bomb 14C Variations in the Construction of Age-depth Models. *Radiocarbon* 47: 115–134. https://doi.org/10.1017/S0033822 200052243.

Grand-Clement, E., K. Anderson, D. Smith, D. Luscombe, N. Gatis, M. Ross, and R.E. Brazier. 2013. Evaluating Ecosystem Goods and Services After Restoration of Marginal Upland peatlands in South-West England. *Journal of Applied Ecology* 50: 324–334. https://doi.org/10.1111/1365-2664.12039.

Griffin, C.J. 2012. Animal Maiming, Intimacy and the Politics of Shared Life: the Bestial and the Beastly in Eighteenth-and Early Nineteenth-century England. *Transactions of the Institute of British Geographers* 37: 301–316. https://doi. org/10.1111/j.1475-5661.2011.00464.x.

Hobbs, R.J., and C.H. Gimingham. 1987. Vegetation, Fire and Herbivore Interactions in Heathland. *Advances in Ecological Research* 16: 87–173. https://doi.org/10.1016/S0065-2504(08)60088-4.

Jacobson, G.L., and R.H. Bradshaw. 1981. The Selection of Sites for Paleovegetational Studies. *Quaternary Research* 16: 80–96. https://doi. org/10.1016/0033-5894(81)90129-0.

Kelly, M., and Gráda, C. Ó. 2020. The Economic Impact of the Little Ice Age. *UCD Centre for Economic Research Working Paper series*, No. WP10/14. http://hdl.handle.net/1019/2649

MacDermot, E.T. 1973. *The History of the Reclamation of Exmoor.* Newton Abbot: David & Charles.

Matthews, J., and K.R. Briffa. 2005. The "Little Ice Age": Re-evaluation of an Evolving Concept. *Geografiska Annaler* 87: 17–36. https://doi.org/ 10.1111/j.0435-3676.2005.00242.x.

Mazier, F., D. Galop, C. Brun, and A. Buttler. 2006. Modern Pollen Assemblages from Grazed Vegetation in the Western PYRENEES, France: a Numerical Tool for More Precise Reconstruction of Past Cultural Landscapes. *The Holocene* 16: 91–103. https://doi.org/10.1191/0959683606hl908rp.

Merryfield, D. L. 1977. Palynological and Stratigraphical Studies on Exmoor. Unpublished PhD Thesis, University of London.

Merryfield, D.L., and P.D. Moore. 1974. Prehistoric Human Activity and Blanket Peat Initiation on Exmoor. *Nature* 250: 439–441. https://doi.org/10.1038/ 250439a0.

Ombashi, H. 2020. A High Resolution Palaeoecological Study of Land Use Change During late prehiStory on Exmoor. Unpublished PhD thesis, University of Plymouth. https://pearl.plymouth.ac.uk/cgi/viewcontent.cgi?article=168 9&context=gees-theses

Ombashi, H., and M. Løvschal. 2023. Anthropogenic Heathlands in Prehistoric Atlantic Europe: Review and Future Prospects. *European Journal of Archaeology* 26: 341–358. https://doi.org/10.1017/eaa.2022.42.

Orwin, C.S. 1929. *The Reclamation of Exmoor Forest.* London.

Orwin, C.S., and R.J. Sellick. 1970. *The Reclamation of Exmoor Forest.* Newton Abbot: David & Charles.

Packham, J.R., P.A. Thomas, M.D. Atkinson, and T. Degen. 1992. Biological Flora of the British Isles: *Fagus sylvatica. Journal of Ecology* 100: 1557–1608. https://doi.org/10.1111/j.1365-2745.2012.02017.x.

Pakeman, R.J., and A.J. Nolan. 2009. Setting Sustainable Grazing Levels for Heather Moorland: A Multi-site Analysis. *Journal of Applied Ecology* 46: 363–368. https://doi.org/10.1111/j.1365-2664.2008.01603.x.

Payne, R.J. 2013. Seven Reasons Why Protists Make Useful Bioindicators. *Acta Protozoologica* 52: 105–113. https://doi.org/10.4467/1689002 7AP.13.0011.1108.

Riley, H. 2014. *Turf Cutting on Exmoor: An Archaeological and Historical Study.* Devon: Hazel Riley. https://doi.org/10.5284/1037648.

Riley H. 2015. *Metric Survey of Little Ashcombe, Simonsbath.* Dulverton: Exmoor Mires Project EAC15. https://doi.org/10.5284/1041867

Riley, H., and R. Wilson-North. 2001. *The Field Archaeology of Exmoor.* Swindon: English Heritage.

Rippon, S.J., R.M. Fyfe, and A.G. Brown. 2006. Beyond Villages and Open Fields: The Origins and Development of a Historic Landscape Characterised by Dispersed Settlement in South West England. *Medieval Archaeology* 50: 31–70. https://doi.org/10.1179/174581706x124239.

Rowney, F.M., R.M. Fyfe, P. Anderson, R. Barnett, W. Blake, T. Daley, K. Head, A. MacLeod, I. Matthews, and D.N. Smith. 2022. Ecological Consequences of Historic Moorland "Improvement". *Biodiversity and Conservation* 31: 3137–3161. https://doi.org/10.1007/s10531-022-02479-6.

Rowney, F.M., R.M. Fyfe, L. Baker, H. French, M.B. Koot, H. Ombashi, and R.G.O. Timms. 2023. Historical Anthropogenic Disturbances Explain Long-term Moorland Vegetation Dynamics. *Ecology and Evolution* 13 (3): 1–17. https://doi.org/10.1002/ece3.9876.

Sasaki, T., N.I. Ishii, D. Makishima, R. Sutou, A. Goto, Y. Kawai, H. Taniguchi, K. Okano, A. Matsuo, A. Lochner, S. Cesarz, Y. Suyama, K. Hikosaka, and N. Eisenhauer. 2022. Plant and Microbial Community Composition jointly Determine Moorland Multifunctionality. *Journal of Ecology* 110: 2507–2521. https://doi.org/10.1111/1365-2745.13969.

Scoble, L., S. Ussher, M. Fitzsimons, L. Ansell, M. Craven, and R.M. Fyfe. 2024. Optimisation of Classification Methods to Differentiate Morphologically-similar Pollen Grains from FT-IR Spectra. *Review of Palaeobotany and Palynology* 321: 1050–1041. https://doi.org/10.1016/j.revpalbo.2023.105041.

Sidney S. 1878. Exmoor Reclamation. *Journal of the Royal Agricultural Society of England* 2 (14): 72–97.

Siraut, M. 2009. *Exmoor: The Making of an English Upland*. Chichester: Phillimore & Co.

Sugita, S. 1994. Pollen Representation of Vegetation in Quaternary Sediments: Theory and Method in Patchy Vegetation. *Journal of Ecology* 82: 881–897. https://doi.org/10.2307/2261452.

Conclusion

Abstract This study has shown that ideas of 'internal colonisation' drove the Knights to persist with the reclamation of Exmoor, in the face of repeated failures. As other recent studies of reclamation have shown, such attitudes also provided value-judgements about what constituted successful 'improvement' practices and practitioners, and who possessed the requisite knowledge. As elsewhere, 'native' livestock and people on Exmoor were defined as antithetical to such ideals, and regarded as a race apart. However, the study's additional focus on farming practices and palaeoecological impacts reveals its blind spots. When the Knights undid their earlier 'colonial' schemes in the 1860s, observers either said little, or depicted the improved financial returns as the final 'success' of improvement. Finally, the study suggests that the history of 'internal colonisation' on Exmoor has important lessons for the future. The need for urgent action to mitigate climate change and secure rapid environmental recovery risks casting external agencies and policymakers as Victorian 'improvers', ready to exclude or ignore local knowledge and practices of landscape management today.

Keywords Internal colonisation • Cultures of knowledge • Agricultural improvement • Ideology • Climate change policy • Ecological restoration • Nature/culture • Indigenous knowledge • Co-creation

H. French et al., *The Reclamation of Exmoor Revisited*,
https://doi.org/10.1007/978-3-031-81658-1_6

By conducting a detailed case study of the Knight family's attempts to reclaim Exmoor, this book has demonstrated how ideological goals were often used by historical actors, not only to inspire their actions but also to measure their success. Our study adds to the growing body of literature that expands our understanding of agricultural revolutions beyond markets, land and wages, by including consideration of the accompanying efforts to control discourse, knowledge and expertise. The expensive and labour-intensive attempts to 'improve' the flora, fauna and people of Exmoor between 1818 and the mid-1860s were the direct result of the 'enclosure of knowledge' by self-appointed experts that had been accomplished slowly but inexorably in Britain since the seventeenth century (Fisher 2022). Under John Knight and Robert Smith, local knowledge and agricultural practice were not merely disregarded in favour of 'book farming'. Instead, the activities of local farmers were construed as the antithesis to 'good practice' and actively harmful to the landscape. The subsequent denigration and exclusion of the locals who had previously farmed Exmoor resulted not only from discourses of colonialism turned inwards but also from ideological interpretations of what constituted agricultural 'improvement' that had evolved and strengthened during the preceding two centuries.

Impact on the Historical Field: Internal Colonialism

As Kate Mulry has recently argued, during their encounters with new landscapes and peoples 'contemporaries continually reassessed what it meant to live a distinctively English life and debated the cultural, political and territorial limits of Englishness' (Mulry 2021). Yet, such processes were not confined to distant settlements across the Atlantic. The reclamation of areas such as Exmoor demonstrates the divisions within the concept of 'Englishness' during the nineteenth century, about what (and whom) to include and exclude. Agrarian commentators, travel writers and would-be ethnographers increasingly depicted the 'natives' of Exmoor as distinct in appearance, speech and farming practices from the surrounding populations of southwest England and associated them more with the 'otherness' of the Irish or the French than with their neighbours in the adjoining parishes. In this respect, despite in-migration and tourism, even by the turn of the twentieth century, the local communities of these distant landscapes had not been completely subsumed within a collectively imagined nation. Yet, by the time Frederic Knight passed the estate to Earl Fortescue in 1897, there were few who would argue that Exmoor was not an English parish. Despite the distinctly Scottish accents of many of its resident shepherds, Exmoor had become environmentally and economically 'English' via the process of reclamation, writ large.

In her recent study of fenland plantations, Elly Dezateux Robson has detailed how the confrontations between locals and settlers centred around differing visions of the fens, 'customary or improved, pastoral or arable' (Dezateux Robson 2024). Although the absence of a resident population on Exmoor weakens such dichotomies there, these competing visions can still be seen in the activities of the Knight family and their tenants. Certain practices were suppressed, when they were judged as antithetical to soil improvement. For example, in the mid-1850s William Hannam was actively discouraged from continuing his dairy farm at Cornham, because Robert Smith and Frederic Knight had decided that dairy farmers were extractive, and 'not improvers'. Similarly, although the estate's settled hostility to native breeds of sheep and cattle was justified in terms of their small size and low productivity, it was also motivated by conscious rejection of Exmoor's past role as open summer pasture for local farmers, because this was regarded as the opposite of improved agriculture.

Yet, in contrast to Dezateux Robson's study of conflict on the fens, these 'differing visions' of Exmoor were not immovable or eternal. Indeed, when faced with dire economic forecasts in the 1860s, Frederic Knight revived modified versions of the 'customary' modes of farming that had been practiced on Exmoor in previous centuries. However, as we have noted throughout this book, in contrast to the well-documented and much-discussed 'revolutionary' transformations, such as landscape-scale drainage, the return to sheep ranching and the acceptance of local tenant farmers was largely a silent revolution. The 'enclosure of knowledge' (by preferring external expertise and livestock) that had been brought onto Exmoor by John Knight and then built upon by Robert Smith collapsed in a few short years. This was not the result of some great act of resistance by the locals nor some fantastic financial miscalculation by the Knights. Instead, it was dismantled incrementally and was largely driven by expediency, but because it was generally at odds with the ideals of 'internal colonialism', it was hardly commented upon, even in the private letters of Frederic Knight. Consequently, although improvement discourses can reveal a great deal about how contemporaries perceived the landscape and its improvement, they can also conceal actual practice 'on the ground'—particularly where this deviated from valorised norms. This is true not only of environmental changes, as we have discussed elsewhere, but also of economic and social transformations as well (Baker et al. 2023).

Although there have been great strides in the study of 'internal colonialism' in Britain over the past few years, our study also illustrates its limits. This mindset clearly shaped the day-to-day activities of enclosers and 'improvers', but its influence was never immutable or overwhelming. Obviously, these discourses encouraged John and Frederic Knight to conduct impractical and overly expensive 'improvement' projects on Exmoor, but neither was a prisoner of them. They rethought or even abandoned these projects when they proved uneconomic, and both were prepared to change course, even if they refused to admit it publicly. Indeed, Exmoor reveals a paradox or delusion within these discourses of 'internal colonialism', and among their supporters. On the one hand, this ideology called for the elimination of local knowledge and practices, but on the other hand, its advocates pointed to their readoption in the 1860s and 1870s as proof of its success. Commentators such as Sidney cited the large sheep herds and the resultant profitability of the estate as evidence that the replacement of local practices and populations had been successful. Yet, the opposite was true. As such, historians of internal colonialism need to be cautious not only about how these discourses influenced the everyday practices of enclosers but also about how these activities were recorded by contemporary commentators and writers. The value of this study's multidisciplinary research methodology is that new, fine-grained palaeoecological analyses provide an important external reference point, or yardstick, against which to measure the impact of this rhetoric on (and under) the ground, decade by decade. While such analyses are only possible in areas where vegetation deposits have been preserved anaerobically, such as peat mires, this volume shows their potential for assessing the extent and impact of supposedly revolutionary landscape change in other historical periods, including the twentieth century.

The study of Exmoor also indicates a gap within our current understanding of 'internal colonialism'. Although the works of Griffin, Arneil and others have detailed the emergence of these theories, their death and afterlife have yet to be charted. Our study has revealed how these discourses were not immortal nor incontestable. In fact, just as improvement's 'successes' on Exmoor were being chronicled by writers such as Samuel Sidney in the 1870s, this narrative was challenged by commentators who privileged Exmoor's remaining 'wildness' and celebrated the failure of farming to 'tame' it. The idea of a 'wild' Exmoor and the description of these landscapes as England's 'wild west' had always been present within the discourses of internal colonialism. However, by the final quarter of the nineteenth century, the debate was no longer about the best method to redeem 'wild Exmoor', but rather about how to protect it. In this sense, the discourses of 'internal colonialism' (and specialised agrarian land use) eventually lost ground to new interests in game conservation, landscape preservation and tourism. Therefore, across the nineteenth century, it is evident that these discourses always existed within, and were adapted to, wider debates about the changing material state and cultural value of Exmoor.

Modern Lessons and Applications of Our Study

In fact, 'internal colonialism' may have had a long afterlife on Exmoor. As palaeoecological studies have shown, the greatest ecological change to the moorland was caused by the vast diesel-powered drainage schemes of the inter-war period. Similarly, conflicts between outside expertise and local knowledge have continued to provoke major moments of protest. The attempted afforestation of The Chains during the 1950s, for example, was couched in many of the discourses of 'internal colonialism' with experts criticising the parochial views of local people (Brotherton 1990; Lobley and Winter 2009; Lowe et al. 1986). Similarly, the later battles between Exmoor National Park Authority and local farmers over moorland plough-ing and conservation agreements have involved debates which have pitted 'foreigners' against 'native knowledge'. Although modern experts in the Environment Agency, Forestry Commission or National Park Authority no longer describe local farmers as 'savage' or 'barbaric', the concern that these folk could be 'despoiling' the landscape with their outdated agricul-tural practices continues to inspire both legislation and action.

'Internal colonialism' created an overwhelming narrative of unproduc-tive wastelands that, with the correct application of labour and capital investment, might make significant contributions to important national agendas, food security and moral improvement of the 'backward' indige-nous population. Today, society is faced with major crises; the insidious threats of climate change, water security, and, in an era of increasing geo-political turmoil, food security press upon the minds of policymakers in Whitehall. Eyes turn once more to marginal landscapes, where landscape restoration programmes aim to mitigate climatic change through securing carbon in peatlands (Grand-Clement et al. 2013) or extensive tree planting schemes (Westaway et al. 2023). External agencies seek to exert greater control over land management practices, via changes in the subsidy schemes available for upland farmers. Concerns have focused on the proposed Environmental Land Management payment scheme (ELMS), which is scheduled to replace the Basic Payment Scheme (BPS) following the UK's withdrawal from the European Union. Commentators have suggested that the new scheme may be catastrophic for businesses that try to maintain existing approaches to upland farming (Case 2024). Farming businesses have always responded to market and policy actors (Hanley et al. 2007) and will continue to do so, but external interventions are rarely met favourably and are perhaps received with hostility. Maintaining a binary distinction between the 'natural' and the 'unnatural' overlooks how our landscapes have changed over time and creates an ahistorical and artificial 'natural baseline'.

As recent examinations have shown, the introduction of small-scale agriculture into 'protected areas' has not only proved beneficial in encouraging collaboration between authorities and local communities but also appears to have ecological benefits (Yeo 2024: 101–136). Without appropriate co-design principles (e.g., in work with communities in Sub-Saharan Africa described in Blake et al. 2018), there is a risk that pressure to address such national, existential crises may drive these external agencies to exert influence over local practice in ways that echo the very approaches that failed the Knights: rejection of indigenous knowledge, and imposition of new ways of working without effective understanding of local conditions. Clashes between local people and 'outside' knowledge have important lessons for modern conservation movements. As Ben Bobowski and Mark Fiege have noted in their study of North American National Parks, the emphasis on 'scientific knowledge' as the basis for conservation has frequently encouraged conflict with native peoples and stalled any form of productive collaboration (Bobowski and Fiege 2023). Instead, Bobowski and Fiege stress that 'elegant conservation' can only occur when local co-operation and collaboration become the central pillar for resource managers.

The endeavours of the Knight family, and the running commentary provided by the national press and agricultural journals, also indicate that even the most fervent discourses and ideologies forged in the boardrooms of London (or on the computers of academics) do not necessarily survive implementation or 'day-to-day' practice. This is especially evident when such schemes are enacted by individuals with little personal knowledge of these landscapes and little interest in, or even disdain for, the customs, traditions and lived experiences of native peoples. Such lessons, as modern ecologists are discovering, apply equally to contemporary conservation and restoration projects as well as to nineteenth-century agricultural 'improvement' and moorland 'reclamation'. Without consultation and co-production with local communities, even the most noble plans to 'save' Exmoor will be difficult to implement successfully, or in a timely and economically sensible manner.

REFERENCES

DEVON HERITAGE CENTRE

DHC 1262M/0/E/20/153 Exmoor Estate Rental Ladyday 1885

THE NATIONAL ARCHIVES (UK)

TNA LR5/1/2 Office of the Auditors of Land Revenue, Account of William Lock, Deputy Forester, Lady Day 1814 to Lady Day 1817).

SECONDARY WORKS

Baker, L., F. Rowney, H. French, and R. Fyfe. 2023. 'Revolution and Continuity? *Reassessing Nineteenth-Century Moorland Reclamation Through Palaeoecological and Archival Research*', Landscape Research 49 (1): 48–63. https://doi.org/10.1080/01426397.2023.2244904.

Blake, W.H., A. Rabinovich, M. Wynants, C. Kelly, M. Nasseri, I. Ngondya, A. Patrick, K. Mtei, L. Munishi, and P. Boeckx. 2018. Soil Erosion in East Africa: And Interdisciplinary Approach to Realizing Pastoral Land Management Change. *Environmental Research Letters* 13: 124014. https://doi.org/10.1088/1748-9326/aaea8b.

Bobowski, B., and M. Fiege. 2023. Elegant Conservation: Reimagining Protected Area Stewardship in the 21st Century. *Ecology & Society* 28. https://doi.org/10.5751/ES-13788-280125.

Brotherton, I. 1990. On the Rise and Demise of Conflict in Exmoor. *Journal of Environmental Management* 30 (4): 353–370. https://doi.org/10.1016/0301-4797(90)90028-U.

Case, P. 2024. Hill Farmers Unimpressed with Defra's new ELM Offer for Uplands. *Farmer's Weekly* https://www.fwi.co.uk/business/payments-schemes/elm/hill-farmers-unimpressed-with-defras-new-elm-offer-for-uplands

Dezateux Robson, E. 2024. Fen Plantation: Commons, Calvinism and the Boundaries of Belonging in Early Modern England. *Journal of British Studies* 63 (1): 30–62. https://doi.org/10.1017/jbr.2023.72.

Fisher, J. 2022. *The Enclosure of Knowledge: Books, Power and Agrarian Capitalism in Britain, 1660–1800*. Cambridge: Cambridge University Press. https://doi-org.uoelibrary.idm.oclc.org/10.1017/9781009049283.

Grand-Clement, E., K. Anderson, D. Smith, D. Luscombe, N. Gatis, M. Ross, and R.E. Brazier. 2013. Evaluating Ecosystem Goods and Services After Restoration of Marginal Upland Peatlands in South-West England. *Journal of Applied Ecology 50* (2): 324–334. https://doi.org/10.1111/1365-2664.12039.

Hanley, N., S. Colombo, P. Mason, and H. Johns. 2007. The Reform of Support Mechanisms for Upland Farming: Paying for Public Goods in the Severely Disadvantaged Areas of England. *Journal of Agricultural Economics* 58: 433–453. https://doi.org/10.1111/j.1477-9552.2007.00114.x.

Lobley, M., and M. Winter. 2009. "Born out of Crisis": Assessing the Legacy of Exmoor Moorland Management Agreements. *Rural History* 20 (2): 229–247. https://doi.org/10.1017/S0956793309990069.

Lowe, P., G. Cox, M. MacEwan, T. O'Riordan, and M. Winter. 1986. *Countryside Conflicts: The Politics of Farming Forestry and Conservation*. Gower: Aldershot.

Mulry, K. 2021. *An Empire Transformed: Remolding Bodies and Landscapes in the Restoration Atlantic*. New York: New York University Press. https://doi-org.uoelibrary.idm.oclc.org/10.18574/nyu/9781479879649.001.0001.

Westaway, S., I. Grange, J. Smith, and L.G. Smith. 2023. Meeting tree Planting Targets on the UK's Path to Net-zero: a Review of Lessons Learnt from100 Years of Land Use Policies. *Land Use Policy* 125: 106502. https://doi.org/10.1016/j.landusepol.2022.106502.

Yeo, S. 2024. *Nature's Ghosts: The World we Lost and How to Bring it Back*. Manchester: Harper North.

INDEX

The manufacturer's authorised representative in the EU is Springer
Nature Customer Service Centre GmbH, Europaplatz 3, 69115 Heidelberg,
Germany. If you have any concerns regarding our products, please
contact ProductSafety@springernature.com

Printed and bound by CPI Group (UK) Ltd, Croydon, CR0 4YY
24/04/2026
02096315-0016